3,00

15—

Gran'pappy's Pistol

SUSPENDED OPERATIONS

From an early edition of *Roughing It* by Mark Twain.

GRAN'PAPPY'S PISTOL

PISTOL

OR

TO HELL WITH GUN COLLECTING

A BOOK FOR EVERYBODY

PARTICULARLY ARMCHAIR SPORTSMEN

A SATIRE ON PEOPLE AND THINGS

IN PART ALSO AN AUTOBIOGRAPHY

REVEALING

A PHILOSOPHICAL APPROACH

TO SOMETHING OR OTHER

BY

DUNCAN McCONNELL

———————

Coward-McCann, Inc.   New York

Copyright © 1956
by Duncan McConnell

Library of Congress Catalog
Card Number: 56-10741

MANUFACTURED IN THE UNITED STATES OF AMERICA
Van Rees Press • New York

To the Fraternity of
Ex-Collectors of Guns
of America and to
their devoted wives, daughters and
sweethearts, including mine.

PREFACE

IN a preface the author is supposed to let his readers in on the secret of why he wrote the book. Usually he wrote it in the hope of exchanging some clean white paper that has otherwise been spoiled by print- ers' ink (the book) for some neatly trimmed pieces of paper contaminated with colored threads and equally marred by green and black engravings. Let's call this his first reason, whether he will admit it or not.

Authors have other reasons for writing books. I have known people—well, one at least—who wrote books, published them at their own expense and gave away the copies to their friends. But these were books of poems. It seems that poets are likely to do any- thing. Other people seem to feel that they become members of an elite set by writing a book. Anybody that agrees with this supposition is mildly loco.

Up until this book is published, I have been a member of a more exclusive circle of friends who have *not* written books. Nevertheless, I have no reason for assuming myself so erudite, because writing is taught

during early elementary schooling—along with reading—and most people have mastered the art in some
measure. Thus nobody has a reason for feeling superior because he has *not* written a book.

It is my steadfast conviction that anybody can write
a book. In fact, I have seen some of the results. All
that is required is a determination to spend an amount
of time—that could be more profitably devoted to
setting-up exercises—to scribbling in such a manner
that the typist can't tell whether or not the words have
been spelled correctly. She can look them up. Maybe
you have handed to her the real job of trying to com-
municate to posterity your world-shaking ideas. I
have had numerous capable young ladies suffer from
attempts to read my handwriting. The most tactful
among them never asked simply, "What is this word?"
She approached the subject more cautiously by asking,
"What language is involved?" By gradual stages she
would thus discern what the meaning was intended
to be and would then search the dictionary to discover
the correct spelling.

Occasionally writers are dedicated to delivering to
their readers some message—a religious or political
theory, usually. Writing of this sort falls in a special
classification and requires years of training in order
to accomplish it. The words seem to follow in beautiful

array; all of the words are familiar—at least in some entirely different context—and one can go along pleasantly through pages of material before crashing head-on into a conclusion. Discovering whether the conclusion is related to anything that came before it or not may require careful rereading of as many as twenty pages. Usually the reader doesn't bother; it is much easier to accept the conclusion and continue.

Of this type of writing there is a special variation, here appropriately referred to as the "pseudonaïve archbaloney" technique. It has been developed with such skill as to win a Pulitzer prize, but an additional useful adjunct is the ability to keep one's name continuously in the newspapers. The technique itself consists of beginning each paragraph in an innocuous manner, like: "All good people believe . . ." or "When I was a little girl my mother told me. . . ." This beginning is followed by a generality which might be true under some unusual set of circumstances for some unique situation, but it can usually be set down in such unobtrusive form as to cause the reader not to think. What comes after all of this is frequently a complete misrepresentation about the obviously good intentions of the Russian delegate to the U.N. or a denunciation of some solid citizen who has publicly demonstrated that he is not readily taken in by this hoax. This, of course, is prize-winning stuff which falls into a pattern with some of the prize-winning "modern" art that we have seen. But then, it is such factors as these that bring people to collecting fire-arms—and possibly wanting to use them on occasions.

I have tried gun collecting in a small way and have probably learned most of the ways in which one should not go about it. Nevertheless, it is not precisely this valuable information that I propose to pass on to my esteemed readers—of which I hope there will be many. If anybody is looking for advice about gun collecting, he should obtain it from one of several authors who have not collected guns, but who have written volumes on the subject. These authors are completely unbiased, and what one must always search for is unbiased opinion. My opinions are definitely slanted and I say: To hell with gun collecting! To find out what Gran'pappy's pistol has to do with it you will have to read the book. Maybe you intended to do so without any further advice from me—now that you are a proud owner of a copy, or at least have a friend who can afford one.

The reader will note throughout the book that the first-person-singular pronoun has been used to indicate the author. This usage seems natural; nobody else will admit that he or she has been involved—not even

Preface

a kitten—so I shall not use "we." My son's dog has tried to inject herself into the writing project once or twice, but then, Wacky isn't too bright and probably didn't understand exactly what was going on. Wacky is a bird dog, and if she knew that the book was about guns, she would be hiding in the farthest corner of the basement. Wacky loves guns even less than I do.

If any confusion has arisen in your mind about my purpose in writing this book, I can assure you that the confusion is intentional. But don't suppose that I am confused. The author is never confused, merely the reader. This is aptly demonstrated by the fact that you bought a copy. Burn it or read it, I don't care!

D. McC.

Columbus, Ohio

11

ACKNOWLEDGMENTS

A NUMBER of persons are due my greatest gratitude. Think of the publishers. They have some money invested. You may not admire their literary taste, but they will surely admire yours—and so do I.

Against their better judgment, several friends at Ohio State University have been persuaded to examine the manuscript. Most of the comments that I do not choose to ignore were made by Everett Walters, Assistant Dean of the Graduate School, Rolland E. Stevens, Assistant Director of the Libraries, and Rosamond B. Robinson, of the English Department. Editorially, some commas were redistributed by Edith Rinehart.

Edgar F. Shannon, Jr.—elsewhere referred to as Cousin Edgar—of the English Department of Harvard University, gave it a light once-over, but did not compare it with any of Tennyson's works, on which he is an authority.

The photographs, excluding Plates VII and VIII, were made by Dan F. Prugh, Secretary, Franklin

Acknowledgments

County Historical Society, Columbus. With the exception of Plate VII, everything illustrated is mine—at least for the present.

Martha Ruggles typed the manuscript. Having survived this, she was able to find a better position—and did.

Among the gun-collecting fraternity, Ray Riling and Herman P. Dean furnished valuable comments on how far I might go in lampooning the professionals without incurring their wrath.

If any of the persons named above threaten me with litigation, their names will be omitted in subsequent printings.

CONTENTS

15

ILLUSTRATIONS

All following page 60

Gran'pappy's Pistol

CHAPTER 1

In heaven or hell,
Nobody can tell
Whether the gun
Was an "unloaded" one.
　　　　　　　–CAP'N BALL

How Not to Collect Guns, in General

THERE are numerous ways not to collect guns. First of all, a person should not merely display a casual disinterest, but should actually be fearful at the sight of a gun. If he shows no fear in the presence of a loaded one, he is a genuine firearms enthusiast and will probably reap his just rewards in heaven or elsewhere. Therefore, I say, where firearms are being handled, always inject yourself into the picture—preferably by standing in front of the muzzle. This stratagem, sooner or later, should get your name into the newspapers. Publicity is a great advantage in this game.

A very convenient place to make oneself conspicu-
ous is at a meeting of one of the many gun-collectors'
clubs. The Ohio Gun Collectors' Association is the oldest of these fraternities, but one for every state is a
goal that is rapidly being approached. Pennsylvania—
a superior commonwealth, rather than a state—had
two such organizations a few years ago, one to the east
and the other to the west. Such an arrangement seems
natural in Penn's Woods, however, inasmuch as the
two districts are separated by a mountain range, and
other natural barriers exist, such as language differences. (I shall have more to say about Willie Penn's
Jungle in a later chapter.) Well, look up your local
gang of horse traders; they are always more than anxious to help the novice. In fact, for a price, you will
probably be able to persuade one of these kindred souls
to part with his favorite Zulu. You will, no doubt, be
fully convinced that he is practically giving you his
right arm or lending you his wife. Actually, you probably would not be interested in the latter arrangement
after seeing her.

How do you contact the local lodge? It really isn't
difficult at all. Read the newspapers. Maybe you do
anyway, but this time look on page 16, if there are that
many pages. These gun nuts were never known for
hiding their light under a bushel. After two years of

carefully scanning the newspapers without success, join the National Rifle Association, 1600 Rhode Island Ave. N.W., Washington 6, D. C. Write to their expert on gun collecting—Mister Expert to you—and ask him how to become a card-carrying member of the local nearest to where you live. Mr. Expert can tell you, because Washington, D. C., is the clearing house for all knowledge. Everything is known in Washington, particularly by cab drivers. If you can't remember the address of the Association or don't want to shell out a few dollars for membership, just write to your Senator. This will produce a delayed-action type of result and shouldn't cost the taxpayers more than $50.00, but it might produce the answer you are looking for.

Having progressed from neophyte to an astute member in such an organization, you will undoubtedly be able to learn some of the trade secrets—otherwise why should you have paid an initiation fee? (This is a good question but one that you might save until you have become president of the local chapter.) You will next learn about the National Muzzle Loading Rifle Association and the fact that their dues also are only a few dollars a year.

By this stage in the development of your career you should have acquired the names of a number of dealers

who publish catalogues for a nominal charge of fifty
cents or a dollar. You can, of course, purchase a large
number of these catalogues—assuming unlimited resources—and carefully compare the prices shown,
item for item. This may lead to a mild form of insanity
if you are accustomed to the thought that prices for
identical items should be somewhere near comparable.
Don't let it bother you. The descriptions may be identical but the items undoubtedly are not even remotely
similar. The principal variable falls under the category
called "condition."

Many hundreds of words have been written about
what "fine condition" should and should not mean. I
shall not repeat any of this Washington prose—not
that I am afraid of infringing on anybody's copyright
—but because it is just like a treaty with Russia, completely meaningless. When you run into the term
"mint," dust off this book and look up the meaning in
Chapter 6. In so doing you will surely reflect: that
bird certainly knew what he was writing about, but at
the time it didn't seem to make much sense. (Incidentally, you will note that I have suggested another use
for this book—to let it collect dust.)

Having allowed yourself to become completely be-
fuddled by the prices and their lack of correlation with
the descriptive terms for condition, select a few dealers

at random and order an item or two from each. Wait expectantly for about a week—always leaving with the wife a few extra dollars to take care of the collect-express charges—and you are surely due for a few surprises, if not shocks.

Once I ordered a pistol described as in "very fine condition," and this, to my way of thinking, would be taken to imply that most of the original finish would be present. When it showed up it had no finish at all, except on some unexposed portions at the breech that became visible after wiping away the fouling. I sent the pistol back with the comment that I supposed that "very fine condition" implied considerable original finish was still present, but that I had not found this to be the case on the particular pistol under discussion. This clown wrote me a letter explaining that when I learned more about firearms, I would understand that some models were sold "au naturel" by the manu-facturers. He apparently hadn't looked at the thing closely enough to discern that blue finish was present where it hadn't worn off, or else he thought I hadn't looked this closely. I suppose I should have replied to his courteous letter by giving him some information on how to make friends and influence people. On the other hand, I had already invested about two dollars in transportation charges on the pistol, and the investment of an additional three cents was not likely to produce significant financial returns.

I had, before deciding to hell with gun collecting, bought one or two pieces by mail. It is, I might add, a display of an adventurous spirit—the kind that won the West, if on a slightly reduced scale. And if you are fascinated by puzzles, you can always hold the description in readiness until the gun appears in order to compare them. The puzzle lies in how anybody could possibly apply said description to said gun. After this you can carefully rewrap it and return it with a courteous explanation that you must have mistakenly had in mind a gun described in a catalogue issued by somebody else.

Sooner or later most novices reach the stage where they have confidence in a few dealers who seem to have a common basis in understanding the meaning of a few four-letter English words. If not, they abandon mail-order collecting and start attending the "shows." Admission to these shows is usually restricted to members—an interesting discriminatory practice that will be discussed later. There are two different ways of collecting guns through the media of these shows. The first method involves almost unlimited financial resources. The second involves already having a collection which includes numerous duplicates—some of

which you could be persuaded to part with as a special
favor to a fellow collector. Don't be deceived by the
fact that almost every item on display bears a price
tag; these chaps are not dealers, in general, but fellow
collectors. Don't ever imply that you regard a fellow
member as a dealer unless he publishes a printed,
illustrated catalogue. He might be sensitive about
his amateur standing, which he lost twenty years
ago.

Getting back to the second method, I shall explain
how it works. (There are fifty-seven methods, probably, but I certainly have had no experience with the
first.) It is like the fellow who had a dog. A friend
was somewhat incredulous on learning that he was
going to attempt to sell the dog for twenty thousand
dollars. The friend argued that nobody would pay
such a price. A few weeks later the friend saw the
dog fancier again and inquired about his progress. He
had been completely successful. He had traded the
dog for two ten-thousand-dollar cats. This gives you
the general approach to the philosophy of horse trading, whether it involves guns or dogs and cats. The
only difficulty is where one obtains the duplicate
pieces to offer in trade in this way. I propose to delve
into this matter also, but special psychological factors
are involved which are related to the inhabitants of

different regions of the U.S. Thus a study of the basic principles of sociology in connection with the collection of firearms must first be undertaken.

It is not necessary to have any collegiate instruction in sociology in order to work out some of the problems in human behavior that are connected with the interrelation between the buyer and seller during the process of negotiations for purchase. Supplemental reading in textbooks on sociology is not necessarily a prerequisite either—though it wouldn't hurt any, I suppose. On the other hand it wouldn't help any, because most of these books don't say anything that your great-grandfather didn't already know in simple English. The sociologist has taken pains to "develop" his area of special study through the quaint device of concocting a jargon that is completely incomprehensible to the layman.

The economics of the negotiation is more important than the sociological aspect. After all, you may acquire some warm friends among gun collectors, but in order not to have these relations too heated, it is best to cultivate these friends among those who like to admire your guns and hospitality. Buy guns from complete strangers is my advice. However, don't buy anything from anybody who seems to be attempting to close a deal before the arrival of the police. This situation could be even hotter than an overheated friend.

All outstanding collectors have a gun or two that belonged to Jesse James, or if not Jesse himself, at least one of his brothers. One should always be on the lookout for such a treasure. A friend of mine who was the curator of a museum bought a gun that supposedly belonged to a person of historical importance once. In fact he paid a good price for it, complete with affidavit duly signed and notarized. He described the revolver briefly to me over the phone prior to releasing a newspaper story on his newly acquired museum accession. "Hold the phone! Hold everything!" I said. "That revolver was first manufactured just three years after Big Bad So-and-So died." The next day I saw Big Bad So-and-So's revolver—complete with affidavit. I had identified it correctly. If any portion of Big Bad So-and-So had ever seen that revolver, it was his ghost three years after he was safely put away where he wouldn't need a revolver any more.

At first my friend, the museum curator, seemed quite undone about the whole business. Apparently, he had paid a good price for some sentimental attachments that didn't fit the revolver at all. And all of it had, otherwise, an element of plausibility to it because the place where he had bought the revolver was the ranch where Big Bad So-and-So was known to have died.

The prize piece in this category is a flintlock military pistol drifting around with *Genr'l George Washington* and *Anno Domini 1776* engraved on it. It is, however, a model that was manufactured after 1810. Most school boys know that George Washington died in 1799, but a few gun collectors don't seem to be too well posted on such matters.

Incidents of this sort might be humorous if gun collectors had anything resembling a sense of humor. But they don't. In fact, at the many "shows" that I have attended I have never heard but one person laugh. This hardy chap almost makes up for the others. Last time the OGCA met in Columbus I was looking for my friend and had concluded he was not attending. Suddenly, however, the air shook with laughter—it is not ordinary laughter, but sounds more like the roar of a lion. Well, there he was, towering above the heads of the crowd, and not more than seventy-five feet away. I have often wondered how some of these "collectors" can make the statements they do and still keep a straight face. They can't keep my friend's face straight.

Returning to the "how" of acquiring a bunch of

ten-thousand-dollar cats brings us back to the question of advertising. This is certain to give you an opportunity to buy guns. All one must do is insert an ad in the local newspaper under *Wanted to Buy* and sit back and wait until the phone rings. Although I have run such an ad for over eight consecutive weeks without the phone's ringing (in this connection), in general the phone can be expected to ring. If the person on the other end is a woman, tell your wife not to hold dinner for you—you can eat later in the kitchen.

After about half an hour you will probably learn that you can see the "gun" at a certain address three days after her brother-in-law returns from a hunting trip, which he might do next Monday or Wednesday. If you find out whether it is a handgun or a shoulder arm, you are probably an inquisitor of the sort that would dare ask a suspected Communist if he will swear to uphold the Constitution. But don't ever sell the fair sex short. Just don't buy anything from them if you can accomplish the same purposes by dealing with a man.

Some naïve acquaintances have suspected that I purchased all of my pistols and revolvers from elderly widows and spinsters. I have never disillusioned them (until now) because so few have been obtained in this way as to represent the exceptions. True, I have gone to look at a few guns in the possession of some elderly females. These trips would have been profitable if an appraisal fee had been agreed upon prior to my visit. Once a friend and I traveled a few hundred miles to call on the widow of a former "collector" who printed a "list of duplicates" at regular intervals. This charming woman said she planned to sell the "collection" as a unit and had arrived at her price by the simple expediency of taking the sum of all the prices shown in the list. (The fact that *he* had not been able to dispose of the items individually at these prices seemed to give her the impression that the prices might be more acceptable if she added the requirement that a person purchase all of the items.) Wine may go with women, and maybe a song or two, but not guns, definitely!

On the other hand, if you are concerned about improving your knowledge of sociology, be certain to call on all women that answer your ad to buy guns. On the basis of the assumption that you don't care whether you buy any guns, you are certain to learn something—whether you want to know it or not. Particularly, you can obtain a description of the ol' gal's father and grandfather. And you will later learn that there is a very interesting gun in the family—the one you came to see would be well worth its weight in junk iron—but the interesting gun is in the possession of Aunt Bessie's stepson who lives in Alaska. For all you know, it may be a Paterson Colt, but probably isn't.

Forgetting the opposite sex—I assume that none of my readers are women—you will undoubtedly receive a few replies from men. Watch out for the chap who doesn't know anything about guns. He probably buys and sells them regularly. The person you want to deal with knows something about guns or at least thinks he does. Never make an offer on anything if you can possibly avoid it. You can't win! If you offer a fair price, it may be three times what he thought it was worth or it may be a tenth of what he thought it was worth. In either case you probably won't get it. If you offer anything completely unreasonable on the high side, you might be able to buy it but this is very poor assurance. If you try to steal it—so to speak— you will undoubtedly not improve your reputation or that of your fellow collectors. The answer is simple; just don't make an offer. Persuade the fellow to quote a price on the thing, if it takes all night. It usually does if he has anything worth hauling home. If the price quoted—three hours later—is what you are willing to pay, don't argue that it is too much or too little.

Just pay the man and then go home and get some sleep.

Surprisingly enough, such quotations are not always high. In fact, in my experience, they are likely to be considerably less than the prices a dealer would charge. Once in a while you will come across a man who has something very valuable—he thinks. In fact he has had offers.... Of course, he didn't accept these offers —probably because financial transactions made during dreams are not binding. Only once have I ever been successful in obtaining a pistol that was originally quoted at some significant multiple of its true market value. I wanted this particular model and suggested that the owner contact me if he would dispose of it at slightly less than half the figure that he had been offered. Two days later he telephoned and indicated that he would accept my offer. This is—surprisingly enough—the only time anything of this sort has ever happened to me. Although I do not close the door on further negotiations, I assume that nothing further will come of the incident if I leave without the gun on the first visit.

One should, of course, if he doesn't want to collect guns, follow the individual ads in the various magazines. Here one will find something advertised at a reasonable price about once every three years. He can send a check to Podunk Center by special delivery only to learn that it has already been sold to a "dealer in the city." Mostly he will see such advertisements as "make offer on this very rare ..." or "highest bid takes this. ..." This stuff is sucker bait and probably intended as a means for compiling a mailing list in an attempt to sell gold-mining stock through a foreign broker. One should not be surprised, after answering such an ad, if he receives a letter from Mexico telling him about buried treasure there. Of course, there is always the proposition about the discoverer being too poor to buy a shovel to dig it up. That is where you come in; he probably needs money to build a factory to manufacture a shovel.

In this same connection I recall an advertisement in one of the better magazines. The item offered was a Sharps 4-barrel pistol—probably called a derringer in the ad—without any statement of the condition. The price, $100, was reasonable enough for a dozen, but only one was mentioned in the ad.

This chapter is merely intended to give general pointers on how not to collect guns. There are special maneuvers involved if one intends not to collect pistols and revolvers or if his particular disinterest is directed to shoulder arms. While no special recommendations will be furnished in detail on the handgun *vs.* long-gun aspects of the subject, diverse psychological, socio-logical and economic factors apply on a regional basis. Therefore several of the following chapters are intended to impart to my readers the wisdom of my geosociological experiences. The novice will be quite surprised to learn that gun collecting is different in the Rockies from in the Blue Ridge Mountains. Collecting bullets also is done under different circumstances in these geographical provinces—in the latter by approaching a still too closely. However, these matters will have to await their appropriate turns.

Unadopted proof mark—being a combination of a reflected interrogation mark, an exclamation mark, an interrogation mark, and the biological symbol for femininity.

CHAPTER 2

Silver and gold
Can make a man bold,
But a little lead
Can make him dead.
                    —THE SHERIFF

The Same, in Colorado

COOL, colorful Colorado is a state—rather than a commonwealth or republic—of many variables. Not more than half of the people are "characters" in the true meaning of Shakespeare, but the other half are working toward the attainment of this role before death overtakes them. Despite the ads of funeral directors on the covers of the Denver classified directory, not all people die within a few years after arriving in Colorado. Many of them are very much alive, and have been for many years, and the fresh air and sunshine have not dimmed their vision or impaired their wit. Occasionally some poor soul finds it necessary to leave the cool, colorful region, as I did, but not until he has become entranced by the coolness, if not the colors. (One winter I don't seem to remember any color—possibly because of a particular type of color blindness as a consequence of snow blindness. After shoveling out my driveway three times in as many days and each time starting with the snow higher than my belt, I don't believe I was much concerned about colors, and the coolness was beginning to become annoying.)

While I never collected guns in Wyoming, a few friends from there frequently came to Denver "on the prowl" for any bargains to be found in the Mile-High City. A particular chap is worthy of mention. He had what seemed like unlimited financial resources, which he redistributed in some very unusual ways. He took a fiendish delight in asking me if I would consider disposing of some item in my collection. Once or twice I did quote a price on something, to which he responded by a lower offer.

It was several years after I left Denver before I ever sold him a firearm—directly. If I had something that didn't fit my collection (particularly, an English handgun which would delight him), I would take it to a dealer in curios and Indian goods where my Wyoming friend always stopped while in Denver.

The Same, in Colorado

One Sunday afternoon, he had invited me to join him over a glass or two in the Ships Tavern of the Brown Palace Hotel. He was relating to me his good fortune in finding at Kohlberg's a very interesting percussion English pistol and thereupon pulled this article out of his pocket. He was apparently momentarily unmindful of the fact that somebody had recently done a bit of shooting in this same pub, and been rewarded for his efforts by having a bottle crash down on his skull through the timely action of the bartender. I had thought that the waiter eyed us rather curiously when my Wyoming friend produced this pistol from his pocket, but we did not tangle with the management. Either they had become accustomed to the sight of handguns or had developed the sporting attitude of letting the customer have the first shot.

He did not reveal what he had paid Kohlberg for the pistol. There was no need for it. I had left the pistol with Kohlberg—with whom I had an understanding about his commission for the sale of such articles. Up until now, it can safely be assumed that my friend from Wyoming never knew that he had purchased this pistol indirectly from me—probably at three times what he would have offered me for it.

Before getting down to the gory details about how

not to collect guns when it's springtime in the Rockies, a little more general background should be provided. For example, many novices will wonder why numerous guns of the area—handguns, as well as rifles and shotguns—are either of English manufacture or are marked with English proof marks. Smith & Wesson revolvers with London or Birmingham proof marks, fine English double rifles, and many fine firearms of all sorts are likely to come to light in Colorado. We shall explore this matter further.

Among other long guns, I once purchased a single-shot percussion rifle with Brunswick rifling in Denver. It was a beautiful thing with a burl ash stock, horn tip on fore-end and ramrod, the finest English engraving, and a single set trigger. The caliber was slightly heavy for a small rifle; it measured .545 and .596 inches, respectively, for bore and grooves. Incidentally, although I took this rifle to Pennsylvania with me, the last I knew of it, it was back in Denver. I sent a letter to my friend from Wyoming a few years later, saying that I was then prepared to accept his offer for it. He sent a check and instructions to send it to a mutual friend in Denver. I have never quite understood the details of this transaction, but I suppose it is none of my business. I heard a rumor from somewhere that the mutual friend was originally instructed to reline the bore for a small caliber, but later he was presented with the rifle.

Occasionally one comes upon fine double rifles such as a high-quality Holland & Holland .375 Magnum that another character brought to my house one evening. He didn't want to sell it; he merely wanted to leave it there. He might give it to me, he stated, but "for sentimental reasons" he could not quite make up his mind to part with it. I knew all about sentimental reasons, so I stood it up in the corner of my study. A few weeks later I phoned him to see whether or not he was trying to be subtle about selling it. No, he did not wish to sell it. Why didn't I obtain some cartridges and see if the barrels shot together?

After obtaining two boxes of cartridges, I fired two shots from the right and one from the left barrel at the range of fifty yards. The three holes cut each other, which is probably as good as I can do with open sights. I called the owner of the H. & H. and told him I had tested his rifle. He showed up at my house an hour or two later, looked at the group of three shots, paid me for the cartridges—for which I was grateful —and left with the rifle, muttering something about its being just the thing for bear. This is as close as I ever came to owning a fancy-quality double rifle of this sort. Frankly, I wouldn't know what to do with it

—never having seen a loose bear anywhere except in Yellowstone Park.

So far I have been concerned merely with some of the habits of the natives of Colorado. They are easy to meet, in general. Once in a while a Kansan may show up in Colorado, but he is quickly recognized and, if you take my advice, you will never go near a displaced Kansan.

Once in my wanderings I ran into an unusual cartridge collector. What an experience! We looked at cartridges for a while; he commented that he enjoyed showing his cartridges to me because I seemed to recognize many of them; then he said, "Do you ever take a drink?" When I replied that I have been known to, he left the room and returned with two glasses and two bottles of beer. I had begun to suspect that he might be a stranger in those parts. First he asks me if I ever take a drink and then he comes back with two bottles of beer. However, while I was opening the beer, he was fumbling around in the closet. He came back with two shot glasses and a fifth. After the second bottle of beer and the fourth two-ounce shot, I decided that he was probably a native of Colorado. He was supposed to leave for Phoenix, Arizona, at 6 A.M. the next morning—except that it was already after midnight. Whether he made it or not is one of the riddles of cartridge collecting that I have never solved.

We should return to the question of the many English firearms in this region. First of all it should be understood that not all English firearms in this country were imported for use by the Confederate States of America—well, at lease not the .375 H. & H. Magnum. (This increment of negative information is introduced for the benefit of persons who failed to read their history lessons in school and have not picked up a book on history since.) I shall have more to say about the War Between the States, but English firearms in Colorado are not directly related to this bit of piracy.

Now it might be theorized that the English were supplying arms to the Indians, but actually the Americans were, so we cannot account for the presence of the English arms in this way. Looking at the matter without any subtle implications, one might suppose that English settlers brought these arms with them. And so it was. These fine firearms were brought to Colorado by the "Remittance Men," who purchased American arms during the cartridge era, probably on the supposition that American cartridges would be more readily procurable than English cartridges. Why these American guns were bought in England—as is evident from the proof marks—rather than after they arrived in America is not entirely clear. Earlier models, particularly percussion arms, were made in England usually, and London Colts are not rare in Colorado.

Who were the Remittance Men? They were second or third sons of prominent English families, usually, who did not inherit either title or land and, as a consequence, were somewhat in the way at home. Possibly just in the way of the eldest male or heir—particularly if they were somewhat brighter than he was. Some of these younger brothers may have shown too great an interest in the village barmaid. At any rate, they were able to receive remuneration—let's not call it a bribe— for leaving England. Many of these stout fellows apparently headed for what is now the Cool, Colorful State.

Mementos of the Tabor era of Denver occasionally are encountered in some strange places. In a second-hand furniture store on Welton Street, I once found an American rifle manufactured in Pittsburgh. After some discussion I paid the proprietor $3.50. He wanted $5.00, but I pointed out that the hammer was missing as well as a few other minor parts. Apparently some boy mechanic, probably about eight years old, had taken this rifle apart and hidden the parts that he had left over in the ash can. Nevertheless, it is a very fine and interesting rifle, made by J. Abendshen between 1858 and 1860. It has a vent, and this is the truly unusual feature which suggests that it might have been made for an Englishman.

I frequently advertised to buy old guns in the newspaper known locally as the *Denver Pest*. This brought all sorts of replies, as vaguely alluded to in a previous chapter. Much worth-while information or "leads" came from friends and acquaintances. Lecturing on antique guns before civic groups, the Boy Scouts, etc., occasionally brought in helpful hints, but not nearly as many as one might suppose.

At an Award Night for the B. S. A. once, I was displaying a few guns, and, among other things, going through the motions of muzzle-loading a rifle. (I might say that I did not put powder into it nor foolishly load a bullet without powder behind it. But it all looked like the real thing from a short distance away.) Finally I put a percussion cap on the nipple and said I was about to aim and fire the gun. It was a good, live, noisy percussion cap and caused plenty of excitement when it exploded.

Unlike most other areas where I have collected firearms, the competition was not extreme around Denver during the Forties. In fact I had, principally, one

competitor, a rather elderly hombre, then. While he
called himself a collector, he sold a large number of
guns, some of which distinctly belonged in the classification of lethal weapons. But I shall not discuss some
of my hazy recollections of one or two visits by the
police, who wished to inquire into the background of
these gats. The Old Boy knew what he was doing—up
to a point—with respect to buying and selling. However, his accomplishments as a basement mechanic
brought him fame. He could take an old, rusty,
beat-up piece of junk and really make it shine. The
chief secret of his success was a power-driven wire
brush. Then he would peddle these "reconditioned"
firearms. I ran into these monstrosities all over
town.

One evening he came out to my house to see a
presentation, all-metal Moore derringer that I had.
The frame was gold plated and the barrel silver
plated, but it also had a special type of engraving
which included an eagle and shield (see Plate VII).
A few weeks later a man who lived in Englewood,
Colorado, telephoned me and said that he had a pair
of presentation Moore derringers, so I went to see
them. There they were, all newly plated in gold and
silver. The person that called me finally admitted on
direct accusation that they belonged to the Old Boy,

who apparently was becoming more playful as he grew older. This and a few other stunts of the same variety finally caused me to wonder if his head wasn't in the same condition as some of his rebuilt firearms.

I never minded a practical joke at my expense, if there was anything really funny involved, and occasionally there was. Another very elderly gentleman— and I can justify the use of this term in his case— pulled several pranks on me. Nevertheless, he did on several occasions prove effective in assisting me with valuable additions to my collection. Although Mr. Thomas—I shall call him that—had retired in a sense, he still retained his place of business—for sentimental reasons, as nearly as I could ascertain. He had been very active in hunting and shooting as a younger man, and was not to be separated from these memories. He kept several very fine sporting rifles always on hand and he enjoyed talking about them. If I didn't stop by to see him about once ever sixty days, he was certain to telephone and ask me under one pretext or another to come visit him. Once I fell into a bear trap. He phoned that he had a musket and two shotguns that a friend wanted to dispose of, so would I please stop by. Never in my life have I seen such junk; he probably searched for months to gather together these items. There was a .45-70 with a crooked barrel and the stock cut off, and two of the worst-looking shotguns I have ever seen. However, one of the shotguns had a cherry stock and a square-back trigger guard. I made the very unfortunate boast that I would put this shotgun into shooting order, and Mr. Thomas had a hearty laugh over the matter. (More will be said about this shotgun in Chapter 7.)

Mr. Thomas had gone through the motions of being quite serious about the entire transaction. He had talked to me for some thirty minutes about these guns without letting me see them. He had said that he wanted his friend to receive as much as I could afford to pay for these pieces because he thought the friend could find good use for the money. Finally, he began talking about the condition of the guns. He didn't really know whether they were of much value. In fact he didn't even know whether they would fit into my collection. The guns kept getting worse and worse, but they were not nearly so bad as my unexpressed appraisal on seeing them. However, I remained as calm as I could, and he finally admitted there was no friend and that he would be happy if I would take them away with me, since they had already served the intended purpose. Well, anyway, he was a grand old gentleman.

In Denver, as everywhere, a few policemen collected

guns. One telephoned me in answer to a newspaper ad. When I arrived at his house, he produced a very nice 1849 Colt. I asked him what he wanted for it and he said he thought it should be worth five dollars. In about three seconds or less I produced a five-dollar bill and left with the revolver. Several weeks later, another policeman told me that some member of the force had asked him what an 1849 Colt should bring, and on learning that it was worth about twenty dollars had said, "I wondered why that fellow nearly ripped the button off his hip pocket getting out his pocket-book."

Denver was a great place for picking up gossip on the rebound. There is always gossip about firearms. A friend told me about somebody who had two nice Navy Colts, Model 1851. My friend said they were nickel plated. About a year later he asked if I had been to see them. I replied that I had thought he had said that they were nickel plated. He stated again that they were plated, but that he felt confident that it was original finish. This, of course, was one for the books —two Navies with the original nickel plating—if true. Finally, I went to see these percussion revolvers. They do have the original nickel-plated finish, both are stamped U.S.N. and U.S., and both have the inspectors' initials stamped on the handles. Their condition is almost new and both are accompanied by the original leather holsters. After purchasing them, I learned about their history. It has been authenticated that they belonged to a very famous man.

As one never knows what he is likely to discover, it becomes essential to run down every lead. All too frequently it will turn out to be a "suicide special"—and a loaded one at that. This always encourages me to get my hands on a revolver or pistol as soon as it appears, because I always feel less apprehensive if I am certain that it is not loaded. After easing my mind in this respect, I always hand it back to the owner for two reasons. First, I don't want him to obtain the impression that I am too anxious to buy it. Secondly, I am curious to see what he will do with it. Sometimes I hand him the cartridges separately and sometimes I set them down a safe distance from the revolver. If the revolver belongs to a woman, I usually put the cartridges in my pocket.

Percussion guns are occasionally bought in loaded condition. I once bought one, a Colt, from a man who lived in Golden. It had powder, balls and percussion caps, all ready for business. He was quite concerned about the revolver and handed it to me in a box. When I took it out of the box to examine it more closely, I thought he was going to jump through the window.

After dispelling some of his fears by explaining that in order to shoot it, it was necessary to accomplish two operations—cocking the hammer and pulling the trigger—he quieted down slightly. But he insisted on knowing how I proposed to unload it. He went into the next room—as I remember—while I removed the percussion caps. When it became evident that I had purchased the revolver, I explained that the easiest way to remove loads from a revolver of this type was to shoot them out. Thus we became engaged in an extended discussion of what happens to black powder with age. Somewhere along the line many persons seem to have acquired the impression that black powder becomes more potent with age. Exactly the opposite is true, but black powder can always be regarded as dangerous, and mechanical disintegration of the granules can increase the velocity of burning. The main question, of course, always is whether some dunce may have loaded a percussion revolver, rifle or shotgun with smokeless powder. (This question is discussed further in Chapter 7.)

All in all, Denver is a very interesting place. If it does not seem to be overly sedate, it is probably because of its growing pains. One gathers from Nolie Mumey's *Early Settlements of Denver, 1599-1860* that it is now quite respectable as compared with certain periods in its past. Dr. Mumey has probably made an impression on Denver. He made an impression on me by removing my appendix. I can say, as a consequence, that a part of me will always remain in Denver.

Cool, if not colorful.

CHAPTER 3

The musket we had
Was not really bad—
It was but a trifle
To dream up the rifle.
—THE DUKE OF
LANCASTER (PA.)

The Same, in Pennsylvania
and Ohio

AFTER spending some years looking at the majestic
Rockies that face Denver, the hills of Western
Pennsylvania looked different. Quite different, in
fact. They looked as though their growth had been
stunted.

Our small detachment of one of the septs of the
Clan MacDonald finally became more or less settled
among the rolling hills in a place called Oakmont,
some fourteen miles upstream from Pittsburgh along
the Allegheny River. Except for the railroads on all

sides—if not down the middle of the main street—
Oakmont is a fairly quiet town of about 7,000 souls,
some of whom are worn fairly thin. There is usually
something going on at either the Oakmont County
Club or the Oakmont Boat Club, if not both. And,
excepting Sundays, a few other spots in the general
area serve liquid refreshments—mostly to transients, I
gathered. The big wheels bent their elbows on the
lawn on Hulton Road (C.C.) or down by the river.

Finding a place for a family of five in such an extremely stable community proved a bit of a task.
Apparently people leave the area through death, a
process which about equals the birth rate. Occasionally
somebody will move from Cheswick or Springdale to
Oakmont, or *vice versa,* but such dislocations are extra-
ordinary and are usually contemplated for a decade
or two before they actually transpire. When we left,
we sold our house to somebody from farther up the
River who had been anticipating moving to Oakmont
for some time, although I dare say not since his early
youth.

For real excitement you always go down the River
to P–burgh. If you go by automobile you will find
excitement whether you are looking for it or not. Driving an automobile in this general area is an experience
that practically defies description, and this statement

applies both in P–burgh and among the rolling hills in the general vicinity. In the hills, most thrills are the result of drivers coming around blind curves at high speed on the wrong side of the road. Here the question is whether one will miss a direct contact by inches or merely by half an inch. (I always missed, but I always had my braking equipment in top condition.) The driving in metropolitan P–burgh will not lend itself to any such simple characterization. One night (or early morning) I was homeward bound on Bigelow Boulevard, not wasting any time at about 60 miles an hour, when something that resembled a Cadillac went by me as though I were going a comparable speed in the opposite direction. When I came to the curve at Bloomfield Bridge, I looked about to see if all of the buildings were still in their usual locations. They seemed to be, so Barney Oldfield apparently had let up on the accelerator after he passed me.

The inhabitants of the area live dangerously—if they own an automobile—and this may contribute to their interest in firearms. A collector's competition in this area is fierce. Even in Oakmont there were several collectors, not to mention those hidden among the hills and in P–burgh. Shooters were everywhere and riflery was a major sport at the Oakmont High

School. My older daughter, Joanne, made the rifle team her freshman year—not that she was interested in shooting, but she was interested in going on the trips that were involved in this competition. (To my knowledge, she hasn't shot a rifle since she fired in the last match with the O.H.S. team.)

Well, as I was saying, the hills are full of guns, shooters and collectors. In this area advertising in local newspapers may bring a response or two— particularly if the same idea has not occurred to somebody else within the previous two or three years. More frequently one obtains information by other means. I spoke about the history of firearms to the Verona-Oakmont Rotary Club once. As a climax I discharged a flintlock pistol loaded with a light charge of powder and paper wadding. I am not certain how many hours were required to clear the Boat Club of smoke after this incident, and I was mildly surprised when I was subsequently invited to join the Rotarians.

The first gun I obtained in Western Pennsylvania was the outgrowth of stopping at an antique shop in Springdale. The owner, a woman, typically knew nothing about guns, but she gave me the name and address of a man who had offered to sell her two guns within the previous six or eight months. Supposing that they were Civil War carbines or beat-up shotguns, I didn't go to see the man for several days, but my curiosity finally won out. One of these rifles was an original Kentucky, complete, without damage to stock, barrel or lock, and in shooting order. The other was a rifle made by J. Ferree that had been converted to percussion and restocked. The stock was slightly damaged but none of the wood was missing.

Negotiations for the purchase of these rifles took several hours. The owner had many questions to ask. Which rifle was older? Which was more valuable? What were the comparative values of the two? Nevertheless, I slipped in a few questions myself, edgewise, and learned that the flintlock had been in his family for three generations, at least, and that it had been in Allegheny County for the same period, but he did not know where it had been made. Finally, after a brief pause in the negotiations, during which I went to cash a check, we concluded the arrangements. I was to take both rifles, he insisted, at a price that had been discussed upward and downward during most of the evening. I had at one time offered him as much as five dollars less than his final price on both, for the flintlock alone, but he was determined that they should go together, even if it meant giving the percussion rifle away.

A few days later I decided that I would clean up

the flintlock rifle to see what it looked like. Three large rags were used for the purpose. One was dampened with water and a mild detergent, a second was dampened with cleaner's solvent, and the third was dry. After about six passes with each of the solvent cloths followed by wiping dry, a very large portion of Allegheny County atmosphere, which had been thoroughly cemented with sweat, was removed from the stock. To my delight and astonishment the original, cherry-red varnish was almost entirely intact. Later I found the spiral-striped ramrod on the inside of the barrel. After cleaning the barrel, patch box, lock, etc., thoroughly, I wiped the stock with linseed oil and proudly displayed it to an expert. He insisted that it was a refinished job. I have never been quite certain whether he accepted at face value my description of the cleaning operations.

The other rifle was made by a famous maker of Allegheny County, but had nothing original except the mark of J. Ferree. When thoroughly cleaned, the stock repaired, and the nipple replaced, it made a trip to Denver with me. I left it at Kohlberg's.

Once in Oakmont a friend asked me to examine his small collection of handguns. His wife was busy sewing or reading and apparently not paying much attention to the conversation. Finally he handed me a

nickel-plated single-action Army that was fully engraved, had a gold-plated cylinder, and pearl grips. I
inspected it carefully because I wanted to be quite
certain. Finally, I told him that Kohlberg in Denver
had sold this revolver, and asked if he had purchased
it from Kohlberg. Mrs. B.— nearly fell out of her
chair. At any rate she was on her feet by the time I
looked around, demanding to know where I could
have obtained this knowledge. I shall never startle the
lady further by telling her that I know who obtained
this revolver from Mr. B.— when he sold it a few
years later. Mr. B— finally inserted himself into the
conversation to the extent of inquiring where I obtained it prior to selling it to Kohlberg. I was able to
give him this information as well as inform him that
the gold plating on cylinder, ejector rod and hammer
had been refinished because the gold was worn
through in spots when I first obtained this revolver.
It would certainly be the delight of any dude sheriff,
anywhere. I have often wondered why I didn't keep it
myself—not that I show a particular attraction for
that sort of thing, but because it was an excellent
example of whatever it is supposed to represent.

The eastern part of Willie Penn's Jungle was
naturally settled before the western part and much
gun trading still goes on in that area around the City

of Brotherly Love. Some very large collections have been assembled there and some of them are still intact, although others have been dispersed.

One of the better known dealers and authors of books on guns is Ray Riling, a fellow who is very easy to meet and very difficult not to buy some books from. Most firearms enthusiasts in this general area know Riling and have seen his tremendous collection of powder flasks—the subject of one of his recent books. Riling collected firearms at one time and they numbered about twenty-five hundred small arms, but when I visited him at 6844 Gorsten St., Philadelphia, he had less than half a dozen on hand, and they seemed to be for sale.

There are a few shops in Philadelphia that keep a number of antique guns on hand most of the time. I purchased a small percussion revolver at one of these stores and discovered after returning to the hotel that four of the chambers were loaded with powder and balls. This is the only time I have ever purchased a loaded handgun from a dealer, but they do things differently around Phila.—mostly the way the same things were done in William Penn's day, insofar as possible.

One could write a book about experiences in Pennsylvania after spending a week or two in the area,

ILLUSTRATIONS
OF SOME TYPICAL
NON-MILITARY AMERICAN HANDGUNS
AND A FEW OTHER THINGS

PLATE I   MULTIPLE-SHOT PISTOLS

Six-shot pepperbox marked *Allen & Thurber, Worcester; Patented 1837; Cast Steel; Allen's Patent.* Barrels 3¾ inches long. Engraved frame. Percussion, caliber ca. .30. Assembly No. 240.

Two-shot pistol with turn-over barrels marked *Frank Wesson, Worcester, Mass.; Ptd. Dec. 15/68.* Frame: nickel-plated bronze. Barrels: blue, 2½ in. Caliber .32 rimfire. Serial No. 125.

Three-shot pistol marked *Wm. W. Marston, Patented May 26, 1857, New York City; Improved 1864.* Frame: silver-plated bronze. Barrels: blue. Barrels swing down to load. Caliber .32 rimfire. Serial No. 1236.

Magazine pistol marked *E. Remington & Sons, Ilion, N. Y. Riders Pat. Aug. 16th, 1871.* Frame: nickel-plated steel. Caliber .32 rimfire extra short. Assembly No. 98.

Four-shot pistol marked *C. Sharps & Co., Philada., Pa.; Patent 1859.* Frame: silver-plated bronze. Barrels: blue, 2½ in. Barrels slide forward to load by depressing button at front of frame, but only when hammer is at half-cock position (on this particular model). Caliber .22 rimfire. Serial No. 21958.

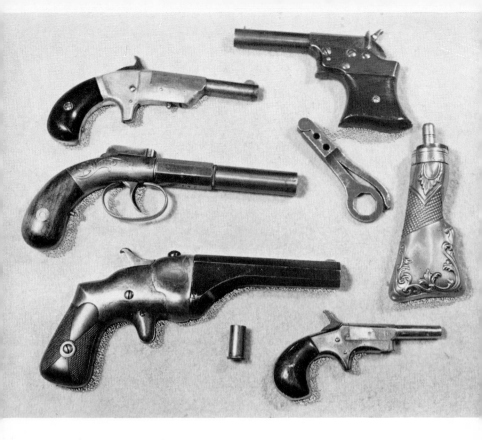

PLATE II   SINGLE-SHOT PISTOLS

Vest-pocket derringer marked *Remington's Ilion, N. Y.; Pat'd Oct. 1, 1861, Nov. 15, 1864.* Barrel and frame blued steel. Barrel 3¾ in. Caliber .41 rimfire. Serial No. 3208.

Cartridge pistol marked *Cowles & Son, Chicopee, Mass.* Frame: silver-plated bronze. Barrel: blue, 3⅛ in. (swings to side to load). Caliber .30 rimfire. Serial No. 3627.

Percussion pistol marked *Allen, Thurber & Co., Patented 1845.* Bar hammer, no sights. Barrel 4 in. Caliber ca. .36. Assembly No. 351. Note barrel wrench on handle of bullet mold.

Heavy-caliber pistol marked *Connecticut Arms & Manfg. Co., Naubuc, Conn.; Patented Oct. 25, 1864.* Commonly called the "Hammond Bulldog." Breech rotates to side to load. Barrel: blue, 4 in. Frame: case-hardened steel. Grips: checkered rubber. Caliber .44 rimfire (the cartridge for the Henry rifle). Serial No. 2930.

Unmarked .22 rimfire pistol. Frame and barrel nickel plated. Total length 4½ in.

(Also shown is a rare copper powder flask of the gunstock pattern.)

PLATE III   EARLY POCKET REVOLVERS

Six-shot percussion revolver marked *James Warner, Springfield, Mass., U.S.A.; Warners Patent 1857.* Caliber ca. .31. Serial No. 7380.

Five-shot, sleeve-cylinder revolver marked *B.A. Co.; Patented April 14, 1863.* (Brooklyn Arms Co.; Slocum's patent.) Frame: engraved, silver-plated bronze. The cylinder consists of a central portion containing five separable chambers or sleeves, which slide forward to load. Empty cases are ejected by a fixed rod as the sleeves slide forward. Caliber .32 rimfire. Serial No. 3115.

Teat-cartridge revolver marked *Moore's Pat. Fire Arms Co., Brooklyn, N. Y.; Williamson's Patent January 5, 1864.* Six-shot revolver using special, front-loading cartridge. Frame: engraved, silver-plated bronze. Barrel: blue, 3¼ in. Caliber .32. Serial No. 5690.

Front-loading revolver marked *Eagle Arms Co., New York; Patented July 12, 1859 and July 21, 1863; Pat'd May 3, 1864.* Small ejector rod behind cylinder removes empty cup-primed cartridge cases. Frame: silver-plated bronze. Barrel: blue, octagonal, 4½ in. Six shot, caliber .30. Serial No. 3742.

Conversion of Remington revolver made under Rider's patent. Requires removal of cylinder to load because of separate plate behind cylinder. Double action. Nickel plated, except hammer, cylinder pin and trigger. Unquestionably made by Remington but unmarked except for numbers: *115* on frame and *1753* on cylinder and plate. Caliber .32 rimfire.

Five-shot revolver marked *E. Remington & Sons, Ilion, N.Y.; Pat. W. S. Smoot Oct. 21, 1873.* Nickel-plated frame, checkered rubber grips. Small ejector rod on right side. Caliber .32 rimfire. Serial No. 889.

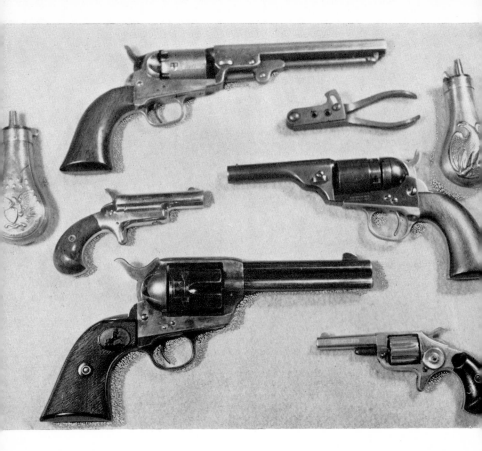

PLATE IV   COLT'S PISTOLS AND REVOLVERS

Model 1849, five-shot, percussion revolver with 6-inch barrel, engraved cylinder and silver-plated trigger guard and backstrap. Marked: *Address Sam'l Colt, New York City* (two lines on barrel) *Colt's Patent* (on frame) *Engraved by W. L. Ormsby, New York* (on cylinder). Caliber .31. Serial No. 83571.

Conversion model (.36 percussion to .38 Colt). This is a typical factory conversion involving insertion of a fixed plate at the breech, alteration of the hammer, and a new barrel without provision for loading lever. The trigger guard is marked *.31 cal.* and was obviously intended for a different model. Serial No. 325671 (all parts including trigger guard).

Single-shot pistol, third model. Marked *COLT* (on barrel), rampant colt and arrows on left side of frame. (London proofmarks on under side of barrel are unusual.) Nickel-plated barrel and frame. Caliber .41 rimfire. Serial No. 32904.

Single-action army model. Barrel 4¾ in. Caliber .32-20 (.32 W.C.F.) Serial No. 306047.

New Model revolver. Marked *Colt New .22; Colt's Pt. F.A. Mfg. Co., Hartford, Ct. U.S.A.* Seven-shot, nickel-plated revolver. Serial No. 51022.

(Also shown are powder flasks and a bullet mold of the types sold with .31 caliber, cased revolvers.)

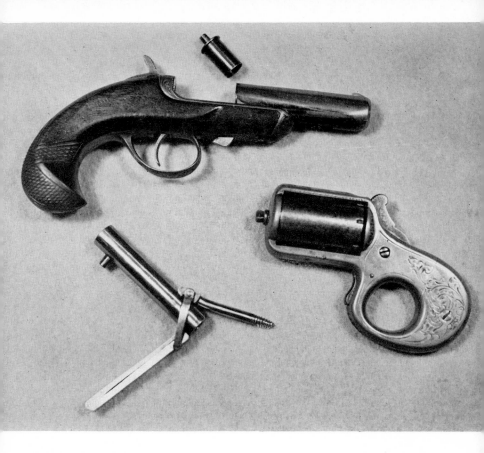

PLATE V   ODDITIES

Combination single-shot derringer which uses .41 caliber rimfire cartridges or an auxiliary percussion chamber (shown). Marked *Williamson's Pat. Oct. 2, 1866, New York.* Flat-topped barrel 2½ in. Trigger guard and barrel housing are silver-plated bronze. Serial No. 753.

 Knuckle duster, marked *My Friend, Pat'd Dec. 26, 1865.* [Reid's patent.] Silver-plated, engraved bronze frame; blue cylinder. Seven shot, .22 rimfire caliber. Serial No. 10645.

Percussion alarm pistol. This device screws into door or window frame by means of the screw at right. When the door is opened the spring (to left) falls and strikes a cap on the tube at the rear of the barrel, thus causing its discharge. While the barrel could be loaded with a blank charge, there is no need for assuming that a bullet was always omitted. This example is unmarked but is similar to others marked *S. Coon, Patent Sept. 22, 1857.* The barrel is 2½ inches long and about .25 caliber.

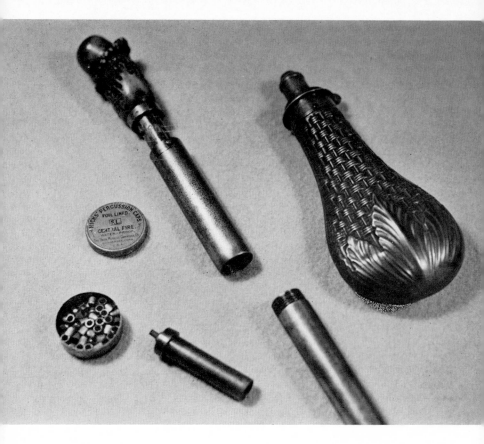

PLATE VI   CANE GUN AND ACCESSORIES

This hand-made cane gun consists of three essential parts. The mechanism
(above) is shown with the cocking head pulled out—after which it is closed and
locked by turning the stag handle. The trigger is a small button on the lower
of two brass bands, between the stag handle and the steel housing. An auxiliary
chamber with shoulder and tube is shown to the left. It drops into place in the
barrel (extending out of the photo) and the mechanism is then screwed to
the barrel. The chamber was probably loaded with shot, rather than a slug,
because the barrel is not rifled. Caliber about .48. A box of percussion caps and
a copper powder flask are shown also.

PLATE VII   ENGRAVED METAL

The central item is a single-action Colt with intricate engraving and inlays executed by the modern Bavarian mastercraftsman, August Heym. The metal handles are the work of another person. (Courtesy of Ray Riling)

The smaller revolver is one of the better quality "Suicide Specials," marked *Napoleon*. The decoration in this instance is comparatively crude—but not too bad for a few dollars. (Photo by G. F. Bateman)

The perched eagle and shield is an impression of the engraving on the handle of a Moore derringer which is gold and silver plated. (When you run out of something useful to do, try to take such an impression from a complex curved surface involving small radii.)

PLATE VIII   A PLATE OF CHERRIES

(Dept. Photogr., O.S.U.)

unless one restricts one's experiences to a very narrow topic like collection of firearms. The longer one remains in this great commonwealth, however, the less one would write because experiences that originally impress one as unusual become more and more commonplace through repetition. In fact, most of the natives do not seem to regard anything about their daily routines or even their speech as essentially peculiar. All, even the small children, apparently can understand at least one dialect of Pennsylvanese. I almost learned to disguise my speech in order to pass for a native. A few simple rules are helpful, such as: (a) select a completely improbable word order like "throw the man over the fence the ball" or "throw the fence over to the man the ball"; (b) end about every third sentence with "yet" and always substitute this word when "now" is meant; (c) learn to speak very rapidly in low tones with the voice directed toward the ground; and (d) learn a few of the words used locally for injection into casual conversation. The last proposition will prove the most difficult because there may be, for many weeks, no clear indication of what such a word might mean, and a dictionary is no help whatever. Some day confide in a native that you are attempting to learn the lingo and maybe he will help you. It should be further explained that the context in which such words are used cannot be relied upon to give any clue to their meaning—not in the Western dialect, at any rate.

The McConnell family remained in the Woods only three years before migrating to central Ohio. For many years I had gone through Ohio, usually as rapidly as the somewhat battered highways would permit, but this time it seemed that we were here semi-permanently. Columbus is a great city. Or, should I say, a tremendously large country town that cannot quite make up its mind whether it wants to be a city or not. The climate during the summer cannot quite seem to make up its mind whether it is semitropical or not.

The driving habits of the natives here, while comparable with those of Pittsburgh and Western Pennsylvania, fall into two distinctive patterns. The high-speed, miss-everything-by-half-an-inch city types are here, as in most eastern cities. But interspersed with them are the ones who move more slowly, meanwhile looking out the side window rather than the windshield, who drive down the center of the street paying no attention whatever to traffic lanes, and turn corners by going completely over to the other side in order to enjoy a larger radius of curvature. The real experiment will be the outgrowth of the mixing of these two types, and it will be interesting to see which survives or whether they will interbreed to produce a more hardy strain.

If gun collectors were plentiful in Pennsylvania, they are superabundant in Ohio. Ohio is a very excellent place to look for antique guns, but, I should add, a rather poor place to find many. The reason for the latter situation seems to be the ratio of guns to gun collectors, which must be somewhere between ten to fifteen guns for each collector, and continues to decline as the collectors increase. In other words, most of the gun collecting in Ohio has already been done, and from here on it is largely a matter of horse trading.

Although one cannot prognosticate that very few items of genuine interest will appear in succeeding years, the probability is steadily declining. Up until this very time I have been attempting to collect guns in Ohio, but they don't collect very well. A few nice pieces have been acquired by horse trading but even this activity seems to have lessened. To the bag of previously mentioned tricks (advertising in local newspapers, speaking before civic groups, etc.) I have even added a few others with far less than overwhelming success.

Attendance at country sales may offer one the

privilege of bidding on a somewhat dilapidated half-stock rifle occasionally, but the frequency with which these rifles appear at sales is a little discouraging. As the bidding frequently goes, one would be better off sitting at home reading this book and purchasing such a rifle from a dealer—if he has any desire to own such an item. I have bought a few rifles at these auctions, but only a few. The weird and wonderful behavior of a crowd at an auction is so fascinating, however, that one will always get his money's worth by attending one of these affairs—if he doesn't buy anything, that is. The dealers have begun to appreciate this psychology, particularly after keeping something marked with a sale price of ten dollars for six months and then selling it at an auction for twenty dollars. After discussing the matter with dealers and amateur psychologists, I have concluded that most of the people who attend do not have the foggiest idea what value should be attached to any of the items, but base their bid on the fact that a recognized dealer appears to want something because he or she is bidding on it. Nevertheless, these auctions are a form of entertainment that should not be missed. Like some of the stuff seen on Broadway, these performances will create for you the pleasant insecurity of wondering whether they are crazy or whether you are.

The Same, in Pennsylvania and Ohio

A few firearms were added to my collection as a result of an article that appeared in the Sunday magazine section of the *Columbus Dispatch*. That is to say, I obtained some leads that ultimately culminated in negotiations to purchase. For several weeks I received mail from various rural areas of the state telling me what was available and suggesting that I jump in my car and run over to see it. Usually it was not quite clear what type of ignition system—on the gun, not on the car—was being described, so in one case at least I drew pictures of flint and percussion musket locks and asked my correspondent which more closely resembled what he thought he wanted me to drive about a hundred and fifty miles to look at. As I recall, I answered all of the correspondence, but went to see none of the guns outside of Columbus. As a result of this spread in the newspaper, a few, but only a few, guns were purchased.

Unfortunately the person who wrote the article, a free-lance journalist, didn't come out any better than I did. He made numerous photographs, including two or three excellent colored ones, which the newspaper did not use and consequently didn't purchase. (If anybody is in the market for some 4 x 5 colored transparencies of handguns, I believe he could be approached in this matter. The potential purchaser will have to show an interest before the colors have faded away, however, and months are now passing into years since these pictures were made.)

One of the neighborhood churches operates a trading post where items are listed on file cards, as well as stand around to collect dust. I requested that my name be listed to purchase guns, although this request was not intended to produce any offense with respect to several beat-up shotguns that were collecting dust there at the time. One day I received a call in connection with this listing, but the woman who owned the arms implied that she would rather give them to her small nephew than sell them for what she suspected I would offer for them. When I saw these obsolete rifles, in rather sad condition, I allowed that there was no difference of opinion between us. We chatted about astronomy for ten minutes or so, and I bade goodbye —to her and the guns.

Some of the dealers in the Cincinnati area seem to run into something unusual occasionally. I have been able to do some cat-and-dog trading with one or two of them, the most recent item of interest being a Walch revolver, complete with bullet mold. The Walch revolver, in case any of my readers are not thoroughly familiar therewith, has five chambers but ten nipples and two hammers, and fires ten shots without reloading—supposedly. There is also a twelve-shot job that is extremely rare. I have never ascertained the secret of where these firearms come from, but I have noticed that they are quite dear by the time they reach the hands of these dealers.

Frequently the suburbs of a city the size of Columbus have weekly newspapers that announce who has gone to Florida. One advantage of such announcements seems to accrue to housebreakers: they learn which houses should be fair game or just plain sitting ducks. Besides carrying last week's news this week, such newspapers often contain ads that are read by the community children who have lost their dog or found somebody's cat. I have run ads in such papers and occasionally received a reply. Nevertheless, one should not expect significant activity from this source. Once I decided to see how long such an ad might appear without any response. After eight or ten weeks, I decided the experience was not worth the expense involved and cancelled the ad. A more reasonable tactic is to run such an ad twice in succession about two or three times a year. The children don't become proficient in reading any oftener than this.

Shortly before midnight one warm evening, the telephone rang and a very-recently-acquired bass voice described in glowing terms a flintlock rifle. It stated that the rifle would be brought to my home for examination the next evening. As is frequently true, I was not able to obtain much information about my caller, but he did mention a street number. The next evening was followed by others without the appearance of the rifle. Since portions of the conversation had sounded factual, my curiosity was aroused. From a friend who lived near the street number—my sole clue—I learned the name of the occupants and also that the family included an eighteen-year-old son. The son assured me that he had not answered an advertisement nor offered to show his father's flintlock rifle to me—apparently he didn't even know who did. A few days later I saw the rifle, but the mystery remains: who first told me about it? Pixies should leave firearms alone.

The extensive shows of the Ohio Gun Collectors' Association have previously been mentioned. There are local organizations also, such as the Columbus and Central Ohio Association of Collectors of Junk Firearms and Broken Tomahawk Heads. I suppose that this is not the actual name of any established organization, although it resembles one or more in several respects. These local boys also have shows, and one can never be certain what is likely to appear, so one attends on the premise that hope springs eternal. At these meetings I have discovered powder flasks that I sold to one dealer, in the hands of another, and priced at three times what I received for them. Incidentally, I also noticed that they did not move rapidly at the new prices.

Although Ohio and Pennsylvania are certainly different in more ways than the techniques useful in not collecting guns in these areas, they have been lumped together because they could not be lumped separately. If the reader can detect a slight partiality toward Colorado as a place to collect guns, it is because he is giving Ohio and Penn's Woods the benefit of all non-existent doubt—probably because he is an Ohioan or Pennsylvanian.

Of my sojourn in the Woods I am continuously reminded. Apparently some practical joker, whom I have not been able to identify, presented me with what may be a life subscription to a weekly newspaper, the *Coraopolis Record*. This piece of serial literature began to arrive a few weeks after I settled in Columbus and has now been received regularly for four and a half years. The great mystery is why. I assume that I once knew somebody who lived in Coraopolis but I never lived within twenty miles of the place. I hope this is all hilariously funny to the chap who paid for this subscription, but to me it makes little sense.

After these casual observations, I shall take off in opposite directions simultaneously, to the southeast and northwest, without going very far in either direction.

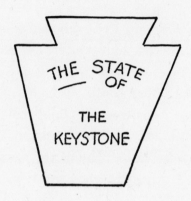

CHAPTER 4

His bullet fell he knew not where;
He didn't even seem to care;
And now, they say, he gets his mail
At a new address: the county jail.
                              –E. X. HUNTER

The Same, in Illinois and Virginia

THE first antique gun that I collected was purchased
in the Windy City at an art-object and antique
shop on Michigan Avenue. It was a tiny Allen single-
shot pistol with a brass frame and a barrel that swung
to the side to load. It would shoot a .22 short cartridge
with a tremendous report and plenty of muzzle flash
—as I recollect—but I was only fourteen years old at
the time, and I may be stretching my memory a little.
What happened to this dainty bauble I have often
wondered. The last time I recall seeing it was while
we were living in California, in the middle Thirties. I

kept it in a cigarette box, and have a notion that some-body helped himself to it instead of a cigarette.

During this early period I did obtain a few other small handguns, but none of them remain. I recall sell-ing the others at one time or another, and while I do not recall the particular circumstances, undoubtedly I thought I had a better use for the money they would bring. Boys of high-school age have unusual ideas about money. If you don't believe this, ask the man who owns one.

Occasionally I visit my parents who live in Glen Ellyn and at such times I usually advertise to buy antique guns in one or more of the suburban news-papers. This has resulted in a few purchases but mostly in some peculiar horse trading. One trade of this sort involved a small powder flask (pistol size). I had gone to see a man whose name and address I had picked up somewhere—possibly in reply to a news-paper ad. He had somehting that I wanted, and I mentioned having two pistol flasks of a particular pat-tern. He asked me to describe the flask in detail, par-ticularly its condition. Finally, he commenced dicker-ing for the flask that he had never seen. He gave me what I wanted and it was agreed that I would send him the flask a few weeks later, after I returned home.

The Same, in Illinois and Virginia

We had never seen each other before but have seen each other a few times since.

From a collector in Hinsdale I obtained an unmarked Remington, a conversion of the Rider's model pocket pistol. This little revolver is identical in every respect with the marked examples and it bears the serial numbers. The man from whom I purchased it seemed to believe that it was not very valuable because Remington's name is not stamped on it. In fact, he was not certain that Remington had made it. I did not inform him that unmarked Remingtons are particularly interesting because of the controversy about their origin. If I recall, he did ask me whether I thought it had been made by Remington, and I replied in the affirmative.

Sporadically, I have collected firearms in Virginia and those portions of West Virginia that should be Virginia—most notably Jefferson County. On the record, the residents of Jefferson County voted to join the newly created West Virginia, but what most history books fail to record is the fact that this was not the outcome of the first election. In the first place, not enough residents of Jefferson County had been disenfranchised, and in the second, not enough residents of Maryland had qualified themselves as voters in Jefferson County.

But Jefferson County could not remain in Rebel territory; it would have been a sacrilege. Had not John Brown been hanged in Charles Town? Had he not become a martyr at Harpers Ferry? Here is a most anomalous piece of history; a man was built up as a hero because of a treasonable assault on property of the U. S. Government. One might assume that even the most unscrupulous historian would have had a little difficulty with that one. But in the days of Uncle Tom's Cabin—which never existed outside of New England, and existed there only in the imagination of a writer of paid political propaganda—apparently anything could happen, and usually did.

At Storer College at Harpers Ferry there is a portrait which is supposed to be an excellent likeness of John Brown. If I have ever seen a portrait of a wild-eyed schizophrenic, this is certainly it. But then, Brown had a price on his head for some of his activities in Kansas before he made a number of miscalculations at Harpers Ferry. Anybody who wants such a subsidized cutthroat for a hero can have him—and Hitler thrown in for good measure.

Beyond referring the reader to the entry under Brown in Chapter 6, and one additional statement, I shall not say anything further about Brown or his weapons. I have purchased a number of firearms in

Charles Town and vicinity, but none of them belonged to John Brown!

In Charles Town, through various family connections of my wife, I have made the very pleasant and profitable acquaintance of one of the leading citizens, who keeps me well informed. He knows almost everybody in the county who has lived there more than a year, and has been of considerable assistance in furnishing information about the location of firearms not only in Jefferson County but in nearby Virginia.

A unique experience involved a lady who operates an antique shop in a neighboring town in Virginia. My friend informed me that she had some old revolvers, so I called at her shop. It was a very elegant place, and most of the items seemed to be priced in three figures. This observation I made while waiting for the lady to appear. When I asked her about guns, I felt a sudden chill come over me until I mentioned my friend's name. That was different. She had discovered these revolvers in a drawer of a piece of furniture, she confessed. She never bought guns, never! She produced them in a shoe box from which she removed the cover in order to allow me a glimpse of them. She replaced the cover and began asking me numerous questions about them. There were the revolvers, two "suicide specials" in fair condition, and a "British Bull

Dog"—the same type that was used to assassinate President Garfield. The last item was in almost new condition.

First she wanted to know how old the guns were. Then she wanted to know whether they were valuable. I told her not very. Then she asked numerous questions about the laws governing the sale of firearms and whether, in fact, these revolvers could be classified as weapons. I answered all of these questions with a definite feeling that they had all been answered before —possibly by her attorney in Washington. After the quiz program seemed to have run out of questions, she stated that she had planned to have her servant bury the revolvers—shoe box and all, I suppose—that very afternoon, but she had decided to give them to me. I offered to pay what I thought they were worth, but she would not hear of it. She hurried me out the door with the box under my arm, apparently apprehensive lest I open it again in her presence.

The "suicide specials" I tore down for parts. The "British Bull Dog" is a first cousin to a "suicide special," but lacks several of the usual characteristics. It is a double-action rather than single-action revolver, and uses the .38 S. & W. cartridge. It is marked with the name *Forehand and Wadsworth,* a manufacturing firm that operated at Worcester, Massachusetts, between 1871 and 1890. I shall keep it, if for no other reason, to remind me of the lady who was much less anxious to receive five dollars than she was to have me and shoe box out of her antique shop.

Another encounter with the feminine sex brought me into possession of a Frank Wesson bicycle pistol, as these things are called. Such a gadget was apparently taken along during the days of the bicycle-built-for-two in order to permit the gallant knight of the bicycle to demonstrate his skill in marksmanship or possibly to help discourage any interference from rivals—I would not know which. I also forget the source of my information that the woman under discussion had some guns, but I believe it was a colored tenant farmer on somebody's place. At any rate, the woman with the bicycle pistol was colored, and I had quite a bit of explaining to do before she would understand why I had come and what I wanted. I started the conversation too abruptly by mentioning "guns" in the first five or six sentences. That was an error because she promptly informed me that there weren't any guns about. It took some verbal artistry to convince her that it might be profitable for her to discover some guns that she had already indicated were not in her possession.

As I sit here sharpening my memory, I believe I

recall who had informed me that she did have some guns. The entire family had stopped to see Rock Hall, where my wife's father was born, and were poking about in the ruins in which some fairly large trees now grow from what was the cellar floor. A few hundred yards away are a group of two-story stone buildings, that were not involved in the fire, where the present tenants live. After we had been there for some time, an elderly Negro approached, and I engaged in a rather extended conversation with him. Of course, he knew Mr. Tom, my wife's father. In fact, he knew almost everybody in the immediate vicinity. I finally steered the conversation to guns.

Such casual acquaintances will not produce much information about firearms as a usual feature. Talking to a Negro in Virginia about guns falls into a similar category with asking the operator of a still where one can purchase some mountain dew—that is, whiskey bottled in hills rather than bottled in bond. Naturally enough, these mountaineers never heard tell of any whiskey's being made in that vicinity, except possibly by their gran'pappy for a short period after the War. They never indicate what war is meant, and it is best not to ask. The answer might be, "the War of the Northern Invasion," if it is put that politely. In such mountainous areas all dates are ante bellum or post bellum, in the same way that modern history is either pre-Roosevelt or after Roosevelt.

One day my friend from Charles Town, who collects old books, and I went to a country sale. Neither of us saw much of interest, but he introduced me to a person who introduced me to a person who introduced me to a person who owned a cap and ball revolver. I called later at her home and was successful in purchasing not only a Colt revolver, but an extremely interesting French paperweight with a colored glass design on the interior. Besides firearms, I always purchase paperweights and historical flasks when an opportunity affords itself. Historical flasks are, of course, ancient whiskey bottles, but they bring better prices with the fancier designation. Even if they contained whiskey a hundred years old, they would hardly be worth the prices charged for them in most fashionable shops.

During the summer of 1951, I worked in Washington, D. C., which is sixty miles from Charles Town. I struck up an acquaintance with a few collectors in the District, particularly with a dealer who had a shop in Bethesda at that time. He didn't have many antique guns in stock but did serve as an intermediary on some horse trading. Once or twice he told me about a collection that he had been unsuccessfully bidding for, and I went to see the owner and had equal lack of success in attempting to obtain a reasonable quotation. During that summer in the District, I arrived at two generalizations: (1) It would be difficult to find a place with a more disagreeable summer climate, and (2) Robbers'-Town-on-the-Potomac is not a favorable place to do any horse trading during the summer. The District suffers from no shortage of gun collectors, but most of them suffer from the consequence of hearing our esteemed congressmen talk about everything in terms of millions and billions, if not jillions, of dollars. To be sure it's only money, so why not?

Toward the end of the summer my wife and oldest daughter drove east from Columbus. Joanne had been baby-sitting in Ontario since finishing her sophomore year in high school. We picked up the two younger children who were in camps near Oakland, Maryland, and all started for Lexington, Virginia, to visit an aunt and cousin. Cousin Edgar drove me into the hills to see at least one gun collection, but nothing of consequence came of this trip. After a pleasant visit, another look at Washington & Lee University (which I attended), Virginia Military Institute (which my brother attended) and a few other scenic spots, the family took off to the southwest and I returned to Washington. It was an eventful summer, which added practically nothing to my gun collection.

The Same, in Illinois and Virginia

Charles Town and vicinity, other springs, summers, and autumns, have produced a number of interesting additions. Besides the several items specifically enumerated above, some rifles have come into my possession, a number of Colt percussion revolvers, a flintlock shotgun, and several powder flasks, including an excellent French pistol flask.

In recent months I have had several letters from an elderly man in Virginia asking why I have not been to see him recently. I purchased from him, the last time I saw him, a very fine Remington over-and-under derringer pistol with pearl grips. This is the model of pistol that was used in the assassination of President McKinley. In reply I always indicate that I will be happy to call on him when I am next in that part of the country. I have no idea when that is likely to be.

Undiscovered Powder Flask

CHAPTER 5

Joe felt the need of a pedigree,
And so looked up his family tree;
He found the tree was sturdy, but
Got hit on the head with a coconut.
–S. A. R.

Gran'pappy Finally Gets into the Act

Gran'pappy apparently was a peace-loving man. He sat out the War Between the States in Kentucky, taking care of numerous women and children—not to mention a few Negroes—while his brothers George, Green and Thomas rode off to the battlefields. After the War apparently he told the Negroes that they might remain and receive wages or leave, as they wished. Family tradition has it that two left, but there seems to be no clear conception of how many remained —possibly thirty. That gran'pappy was a sensitive man is implied by the fact that particular note was taken of the two that left.

Gran'pappy's Pistol

Isaac Wilson Duncan, gran'pappy to me, was born in 1835 at Bardstown, Kentucky, and married Susan Weisiger Lee, of Danville, in 1859. Appropriately enough, he was named after Isaac Wilson, his gran'pappy on his mother's side, just as I was named after gran'pappy on my mother's side of the family. The Spanish have a different way of doing it. They select a given name, say Carlos. If the father is Martinez and the mother's surname is Gonzales, then Carlos Martinez Gonzales is our boy. By the time the succession takes in another generation, the wife of grandfather Martinez and the father of grandmother Gonzales may have entered the picture, not to mention a few additional given names that came from almost anywhere.

Gran'pappy had a faculty for wandering around. After the War he went to Independence, Missouri, in 1873 or thereabouts, and took to raising shorthorn cattle, sheep, hogs and saddle horses from Kentucky stock, in addition to grain farming on a thousand acres. However, he didn't stay there forever, either. By 1887 he had moved on to Fayetteville, Arkansas, where some of his numerous children attended the University. He became interested in lead and zinc deposits and bought some 1,200 to 1,400 acres of mountain land in Marion County, on which I hope to go bear hunting before I die. This land is probably better for bear hunting than for mining anything, but some of gran'pappy's children thought so little of it for either purpose that they disposed of it years ago by the simple gimmick of not paying taxes.

In a few respects I probably resemble gran'pappy. I sat out World War II. This was not, however, so much my idea as it was that of Uncle Samuel. I was working for a governmental agency in Denver at the time, and attempted to procure one of the numerous "specialist" commissions that were being made available to persons with special talents. Whether I lacked the special talents or lacked friends in the right places, I sat out the war and never did anything more exciting than dismantle enemy ordnance equipment that included high explosives—as a civilian. Whether I would have received the Purple Heart decoration posthumously is a question that was never resolved, fortunately. Like gran'pappy, who seems to have escaped from the Land of the Colonels without any military title whatever, I was never troubled with any military decorations. So, if I am stoop-shouldered, it is not from the weight of medals.

Unlike gran'pappy, I did receive a brevet commission—not as a colonel, as a second lieutenant in the Illinois National Guard. You didn't know that they gave brevet commissions of such low rank? Neither did I until I received one, but I don't believe they made a special dispensation in my case. More likely this rank was a clear indication of what was thought of my military attainments—a sort of left-handed compliment, as it were. However, at the time I thought it was grand, and I still have it—complete with large gilt seal and red, white and blue ribbon. It is indeed an impressive document if one does not notice "second lieutenant."

Although gran'pappy was named for his gran'-pappy on his mother's side, he had, of course, another gran'pappy, Thomas Duncan, also of Nelson County, Kentucky. Thomas Duncan, whose combination of names keeps cropping up in subsequent generations, married Mary Green, daughter of Levin Green, Pfc. in the Revolution. Particular mention of Green is made because very little subsequent attention has been given to privates in any war. Gran'pappy's wife, Susan Weisiger Lee, also had a great-grandfather, George Lee I, who was a private in said conflict. There must have been something distinctive about him also, because more of the sixth-generation male ancestors seem to have been officers.

The father of Thomas Duncan was Coleman Duncan, who seems to have no military record, but mention of him is necessary to get the Duncans out of Nelson County, Kentucky—in the reverse gear, so to speak. He moved there from Westmoreland County, Virginia. Where he came from before that does not seem clear from the records at my disposal but, from the name, it seems safe to assume that he was not too far removed from the Highlands of Scotland. It does not require much imagination to visualize gran'pappy's gran'pappy's gran'pappy as one of those "wilde Highland men" wearing a red-and-white-striped, green kilt of the Duncan tartan, together with sporran, dirk and pistols. Judging from what went on in the Highlands during the early 1700's, this fellow probably was not as peace-loving as some of his descendants —or, if he was, that was adequate reason for leaving Scotland.

Gran'pappy had a pistol—probably because it was a fashionable thing to have around in those days. His wife, Susan, discharged it on one occasion. It seems that an itinerant wool buyer—the probable gran'pappy of numerous modern house-to-house peddlers —showed up once too frequently. As is usual under such circumstances, reports differ as to whether the pistol was pointed toward the wool buyer or toward the sky at the time it was discharged. It is surmised, however, that the fellow left—without wool. This incident is mentioned merely in order to substantiate my theory that firearms are far more dangerous in the hands of the fair sex. What a woman is shooting at may be in no immediate danger, but nothing else in any direction can be considered immune.

Gran'pappy had a glass eye, but he didn't let it keep him from being an excellent pistol shot. One dark night he rode out on horseback to attend to a dog that had been chasing his sheep. He fired his pistol in the direction of the dog's bark and killed the beast. It was good shooting even for a person without a glass eye.

The device under consideration is a Colt percussion revolver, sometimes called the New Model Police Pistol or Model of 1862. In those days it was a formidable weapon, capable of producing a bad case of lead poisoning. When last seen it was in the hands of my Uncle Cameron, who will pass it on to his son, Thomas Lee. Both of these Duncans are surgeons, and probably have no more need for a percussion revolver than I have for another one. But maybe it is just as well that it has been kept out of feminine hands.

John William McConnell, gran'pappy on pappy's side, should have owned a small arsenal, living as close to Indian Territory as he did. He did not participate in the War Between the States even as a drummer boy because he was not born until 1855. His father, Samuel C., volunteered and served as a cavalry soldier from November, 1863, until the close of the war; and he should have carried a pistol of some sort during this period, but later generations must have had other things to think about because nobody seems to know what kind of a contraption it was. The arms of Confederate soldiers being what they were, it might have been almost anything—even a flintlock.

Gran'pappy was a medical man, as is his son, my Uncle Samuel Paul, and presumably any pistols would have gone with the medicine again. Uncle S. Paul's son might have a traditional claim to such armament, but I suspect he is fairly familiar with more efficient weapons. He is an officer in the Air Force—a major general or something, but not a "just plain" general with four stars. There are indications that gran'pappy had numerous muzzle-loading rifles, but there are no recollections of any type of pistol. Possibly the rifles were donated to a scrap drive at one time or another; they don't seem to be around.

John William's wife, Sarah, was the daughter of a Presbyterian clergyman who attempted to minister to the Indians—with what success we can hardly guess. The minister's name was Nathaniel Baker McNabb, and his wife's maiden name was Isabella

McClure, from whose father my brother acquired his second given name. David McNabb, gran'pappy of Nathaniel Baker McNabb, was a captain of Tennessee Militia, and in 1780 was fighting an earlier generation of Indians than his grandson later ministered to in Arkansas. Further details about the McConnells, McNabbs, and McClures would undoubtedly confuse the reader—I am almost confused myself. A few generations earlier we would surely find them all feuding in the Highlands, and there we shall leave them.

It makes no difference which gran'pappy is considered; I don't have gran'pappy's pistol. So that's that.

CHAPTER 6

In school his spelling didn't please,
He couldn't learn his ABC's,
But later he knew wealth and fame,
And now the new school bears his name.
—L. I. TERATE

The ABC of It

ON the slim possibility that I may have employed a
technical term or two in the preceding chapters—
I have deliberately avoided all attempts to impress the
reader with my superior knowledge of such matters—
it seems appropriate to supply a few definitions. In
other words, before anybody can accept the statement, "to hell with gun collecting," he may wish to
know specifically what is being damned. He may even
wish to know why. I shall assist him further in these
matters, if he didn't know all of these answers from
the beginning.

It will be assumed that the reader is not a dyed-in-
the-wool collector, or even a novice that could become

highly enthusiastic with a little prompting—this is not for him. He may know something about the subject and be interested in knowing more. This fact could not be used as legal evidence that he is potentially dangerous, although it may set some of his friends to wondering.

The reader, of course, is supposed to have some idea of what it is all about from more complete and more elementary treatises on the subject. Therefore, one must not expect the same precision—nor indeed the same dullness—that he might discover elsewhere. Anything resembling what might be found in an encyclopedia is purely coincidental. If any reader feels that his intelligence has been insulted, this merely proves that some people are more sensitive than others.

ANTIQUE—When applied to guns it usually means anything that is in bad condition or for which it is difficult to get ammunition.

ARMY—Slang for a pistol or revolver that was or could have been used by the Army, usually .44 caliber or greater. There probably is an upper limit to the caliber, but I have not undertaken appropriate research to discover what it is.

ASSEMBLY NUMBERS—Some handguns, and to a certain extent rifles, do not have serial numbers but merely assembly numbers, *i.e.,* numbers that were put on the parts during the manufacturing process in order to indicate which parts were intended to fit together. On Colts, which have serial numbers, the last few digits of the serial numbers usually served as assembly numbers.

AUTHENTIC—An adjective used by gun collectors and dealers in much the same way as the Russians use the word "democracy."

AUTHORITY—"A little knowledge is a dangerous thing," and this is the fellow who can prove it.

AUTO—It could mean an automobile but more likely refers to a semiautomatic pistol. (Slang, vulgar.)

BARREL—Something the local knights of the round table snitched crackers from while solving the world's problems in the general store. See also LOCK.

BASEMENT MECHANIC—A craftsman, frequently all too skillful at reconversion (percussion back to flint) and other modifications which escaped the attention of the original makers. Application of numerous "silver" inlays to Kentucky rifles falls in this category and suggests that basement mechanics may be as early in development as basements. Contemporary acquaintances sometimes rechamber .32-20 single-action Colts to take WW II carbine cartridges. In this case the punishment will likely fit the crime.

BEALS—A fellow once employed by the Remington Co.

BENCH REST—A method for shooting with the rifle prone and the shooter in a more comfortable position. The rifle, however, is not rigidly fixed to the heavy bench and can be removed from the latter—if not by one man, certainly by two.

BIRD DOG—A semidomesticated animal that is supposed to be able to distinquish between a quail and a rabbit. See also WACKY.

BISLEY—Shooting range in Merry England. Also a model of Colt's single-action revolver.

BLUNDERBUSS—Translated from the Dutch it means thunder box.

BOOTLEG—Applied to a pistol that looks more like a dog's leg. Supposedly these things were carried in the owner's boot. (I see no reason even for owning one—much less carrying it.)

BORE—There are two classes: small bore and large bore, the dividing line being a diameter of .25 inches or a waistline of 36 inches.

BROTHERLY LOVE, CITY OF—Philadelphia, believe it or not. Several famous makers of firearms were in on this brotherly love business.

BROWN, JOHN—A scoundrel who accepted financial support from certain warlike interests in New England in an attempt to start a small civil war of his own. If all of the firearms that belonged to John Brown were put end to end, they would extend as far as the liars that own them.

BRUNSWICK—A style of rifling in which an equatorial belt on the ball fits into two grooves in the bore. Used largely, but not exclusively, on English military arms.

BUFFALO BILL—Billboard name of William Cody who acted as provisioner for U. S. troops before he became associated with a traveling show. Here again—like John Brown—is a man who must have owned more firearms than the U. S. did at the close of the Civil War.

BULL—Slang for bull's eye. Paternal moose, elk, etc. Something contributed verbally by shooters, hunters, collectors, *et al.*

BULLET—What comes out of the muzzle when a gun is discharged. (This is put in merely to fill space. If you don't know what a bullet is, don't read this book any further.)

BUREAU DRAWER—Term applied to condition of firearms that have been kept in this place or in an attic trunk for almost their entire existence.

CALIBER—May be the diameter of the bore of a rifle or pistol, but more often merely a numerical designation to indicate a particular cartridge. For modern or semi-modern, non-wildcat varieties consult the titles shown in the bibliography. For earlier varieties consult several good libraries on the subject. (If you find what you are looking for, let me know where.)

CANE GUN—A device for getting within can't-miss range without causing apprehension on the part of the intended victim. (See Plate VI.)

CARBINE—An arm similar to a rifle but with shorter barrel, manufactured in diverse styles and large numbers for use in the Civil War. Collecting these things is like collecting cartridges—there is probably an end to it somewhere, but where is a little uncertain. When driven muzzle first into the ground these things will cause dogs to detour from a path through your garden, if closely spaced.

CARTRIDGES—See book with this title by Logan. See also CALIBER.

CHARCOAL BURNER—Affectionate term applied to gear for burning black powder by persons afflicted by this disease. Also a person suffering from the hangover of shooting muzzle loaders.

CHERRY—A tool used to cut bullet molds. In the early days, a round cutting tool about the size of a cherry. (See Plate VIII.)

COLLECTOR—A dealer that is trying to preserve his amateur standing, but lost it the minute that he obtained a Federal license.

COLT—A baby horse. Also a man with first name of Samuel, who dreamed about things going around and around. Incidentally, he did not invent the revolver, although he invented neat devices for obtaining government contracts.

COLT HAPPY—A blissful state of some beginners who think they will become Colt collectors. If they have an overstuffed bank account—five figures, at least—and plan to invest it in Colts, they probably can obtain most of the representative models and a few variations of the common ones.

CONVERSION—A device for getting rid of parts for percussion revolvers after leading manufacturers had decided that cartridge firearms were here to stay, *i.e.,* after the Rollin White patent expired.

CROCKETT, DAVY—Decades ago a frontiersman. To-day, a 'coonskin cap atop a small boy or girl—the sex of the animated hat tree does not seem to play any part in the game.

CUP PRIMED—One of several special types of cartridge for loading revolver cylinders from the front end. See CARTRIDGES; see Logan; or just see a good TV program.

CUSTER—In martial circles, the principal developer of the tactical error in Indian warfare.

CUTLASS PISTOL—An all-purpose tool for hunting, in season, and for chopping wood, out of season.

DAMASCUS BARRELS—Steel, iron, or both, forged to form a tube of laminated metal for barrels. Also a finish that creates the appearance of fabrication by such a process. Do not shoot modern, long-range cartridges in shotguns with Damascus barrels. A friend who would not heed this advice finally informed me: "You were right. Last week end my gun blew up." He was fortunate in being able to laugh about it.

DEALER—A chap who admits he sells as well as buys. See also COLLECTOR and HORSE TRADER.

DERINGER—A fellow named Henry who resided in the City of Brotherly Love. Also a pistol made by same, or—with various spellings—a pistol not made by same, but by some sharpster who was attempting to misrepresent his product. Of late, a term loosely applied to anything that isn't either a revolver or a semiautomatic pistol and is less than 8 inches long.

DOUBLE GUN—Shotgun with two barrels.

DOUBLE RIFLE—Rifles with two barrels were not manufactured extensively in America, but very fine English and occasionally Continental double rifles are seen. Some persons have these rebored to 410 gauge in order to obtain a poor shotgun from an excellent rifle. They should have their heads rebored; it would do them more good.

DRAGOON—A mounted soldier. Also an oversize revolver carried by the horse in addition to the soldier. Good horses were capable of carrying a pair of these pistols.

EJECTOR—A device for throwing cartridge cases out of the breech of a firearm. (This is included so that readers will not suppose that my alphabet does not contain "e".)

FALSE MUZZLE—An extension of the barrel used during loading.

FG, FFG, FFFG—Sizes of black powder, coarse to fine, respectively.

FINE CONDITION—Means almost anything.

FLINT—A silica mineral used for making sparks by striking against steel.

FRONTIER—A term applied to revolvers by a novice who doesn't know the appropriate terminology. It may mean a single-action Army Colt, a double-

action Colt or any of several Remington or Smith
& Wesson revolvers. (Usually not applied to semiautomatic pistols.)

GAS PIPE—An uncomplimentary term applicable to
some other shooter's muzzle-loading rifle or pistol.

GAT—A term used by F. Theodore Dexter to indicate
a handgun. Also used by hoodlums with the same
meaning.

GAUGE—The number of lead balls to the pound before the pound was standardized as a unit of weight.

GUN—A general term frequently used by persons
quite unfamiliar with such terms as pistol, revolver,
rifle, etc. When used by a woman, it has a very
precise meaning—exactly what she has in mind.

GUNMAKER—A person listed in any of several books
on gunmakers, whether, in fact, he ever did anything other than operate a retail store in which guns
were sold along with jewelry, general hardware, etc.

GUNSMITH—Supposedly a person who repairs or
manufactures guns, but the term is used very
loosely. See GUNMAKER and BASEMENT MECHANIC.

HAND CANNON—A firearm that is not supported on a
carriage with wheels. A none-too-affectionate name
for the .45 caliber semiautomatic pistol, Model 1911.

HARPERS FERRY—Sleepy village at the confluence of
the Shenandoah and Potomac rivers. Formerly the

site of U.S. armory which was captured by John Brown. Location at one time of the Hall Rifle Works.

HARTFORD—City in Connecticut. Applied to Colt percussion revolvers that are stamped with this address. (Other Colt revolvers are marked Paterson; New York City; London; and New York, U.S. America.)

HAWKEN—The surname of two brothers who made rifles, chiefly at St. Louis. Although there have been better rifle makers, none have had better press agents—some of whom are still with us.

HIDDEN LOAD—The one gran'pappy put in the gun but didn't mention in his will. The discoverer of such a load sometimes does not live to describe his discovery to others.

HORSE TRADER—The character who traditionally aspires to trade a pocketknife for a house and lot. (In this day and age he might never have seen a horse.)

INLAYS—Embellishments of metal—rarely silver but usually described as such—on the stock of a rifle. Frequently the handiwork of somebody other than the original maker.

INVENTOR'S MODEL—Sometimes a contrivance which embodies new ideas and is related to a patent application. More likely the product of a basement mechanic whose only invention is a method for putting together an assortment of parts from standard models.

IRON—Metal used for early rifle barrels rather than steel. (It is quite easily cut by tools, when pure.)

KENTUCKY—A fullstock, flintlock rifle of the type used in Kentucky Territory—made anywhere, including Penn's Woods.

KNIFE PISTOL—A pistol with retractable or stationary blade—usually more suited to sharpening pencils than chopping wood. Compare CUTLASS PISTOL.

KNUCKLE DUSTER—A type of oddity, the maker of which was apparently willing to admit that it could be more lethal if you hit somebody with it than if you relied on its use as a firearm. (See Plate V.)

LAMINATED STEEL—See DAMASCUS BARRELS.

LANCASTER—Town in Penn's Woods where, or near where, all knowledge concerning manufacture of rifles in America supposedly originated. Rifles also originated there—as they did in many other places, including New England, North Carolina, Virginia and, later, Ohio.

LIGHTNING—Name applied to a slide-action Colt rifle and also to an early double-action Colt revolver with a very tricky and none-too-sturdy mechanism.

LOADED—What a gun never was, up until it went off. Sometimes also applied to persons or to questions. In general, a term applicable to anything potentially dangerous as a consequence of being full of something.

LOCK—A portion of the expression, "lock, stock and barrel" which I have seen quoted as "lock, stock and hogshead." Supposedly a hogshead would describe what substitutes for a barrel on a bench rifle, if the latter quotation makes any sense at all.

MAGGIE'S DRAWERS—A less-than-subtle signal that the shooter missed the target.

MARTHA—My secretary. Her husband may be a Moose or Elk, but she's a dear.

MATCHLOCK—Type of ignition used to limited extent by early settlers along Atlantic Coast.

MAYNARD—A dentist of Robbers'-Town-on-the-Potomac who invented rolls of caps such as are now used in toy cap pistols. He had in mind their use—in dry weather—on more businesslike firearms.

MINIÉ BALL—Type of bullet used in the Civil War and invented by a French officer with this name.

MINT—Where coins are minted and stored. Meaningless term sometimes applied by overzealous dealers who wish to imply a condition of newness such as that possessed by a coin that has just left the mint. (Guns are not minted and therefore cannot be in mint condition any more than unused brains can be in mint condition.)

MIXED NUMBERS—An honest admission that the parts involved did not originally belong together and that the gun was assembled from miscellaneous, salvaged parts. However, factory-converted Remington handguns usually have an original number and a conversion number. Factory refinished Colt handguns may have a second number—usually only on concealed parts—in addition to the original serial number.

MUFF PISTOL—Tiny pistol supposedly carried inside a woman's muff when women had such things and when it was ladylike to carry them. ("Them" refers to muff, pistol or both.)

MULE EAR—Applies to rifles having two barrels (over-under) and two hammers that cock outward to the side, making an angle suggestive of the ears of a mule or a jack rabbit.

MUSEUM PIECE—Descriptive term comparable to "modern" when used in front of "art." Frequently used when nothing else favorable could possibly be said about the subject. It is not a misrepresentation in the technical sense, however, because anything can be seen in a museum—particularly a private one.

MUZZLE—Snout of dog or snout of gun, or something that goes on either. See FALSE MUZZLE.

NAVY—A pistol or revolver which was used by the Navy or which the manufacturer hoped might be used by the Navy. It is a smaller caliber, in general, than the Army of the same vintage, *i.e.,* .36 rather than .44, for example. (I have never been able to analyze the thinking behind these differences. It could be that the Navy personnel were better marksmen and therefore figured their pistols didn't need to throw something the size of a baseball, or possibly the smaller caliber made them better marksmen. Obviously there are several ways of approaching any problem. And then there is the Army way.)

NIMROD—Grandson of Ham, who was a mighty hunter. In present usage sometimes just plain ham.

NIPPLE—A tube on which the percussion cap explodes —sometimes firing the charge in the barrel as a consequence. All discharges in a revolver do not necessarily take place through the nipple, however. Three chambers of a revolver can fire simultaneously without the cap or nipple being directly involved for more than one chamber. (If you don't believe this, you haven't become acquainted with black powder under diverse circumstances.)

NORTH, S.—Maker of flintlock firearms for U.S. Government.

NOTCHES—Mutilations on the grip of a revolver which was supposedly possessed by some desperate outlaw. More frequently they were added by a small boy with a new pocketknife and a vivid imagination. Anybody wishing to detract from the value of handguns can accomplish his purpose in a few minutes by putting notches on the handle. Where the myth started that these outlaws couldn't remember small numbers, and had to rely on notches on their revolver handles to keep track of deceased friends, does not seem to be known. Surely most of these desperadoes could count as high as six, and inasmuch as I have never seen more than six notches, their supposed purpose doesn't seem reasonable, particularly since nobody was likely to examine the outlaw's revolver closely while he was alive. After his death, of course, the notch supposedly didn't go on his gun anyway.

I had at one time thought of putting notches on the grips of my Colt Woodsman, where they would have kept score on jack rabbits, but here each notch would have indicated ten such encounters—I can keep track of numbers less than ten by remembering a certain number of fingers.

OFFHAND—Firing from a standing position, something which is almost impossible to accomplish with some heavy-barrel rifles. See BENCH REST.

ORIENTAL—This term is frequently applied by a dealer to an arm that can't be identified as to origin. Frequently a five-dollar word meaning a piece of junk.

ORIGINAL—Means without benefit of a basement mechanic. A term applied loosely with respect to finish. For example, "80 per cent original finish" may mean that not more than 20 per cent of the exterior is badly rusted. *N.B.:* Chromium plating was not introduced during the period of the percussion revolver, so that chrome plating cannot be original finish on percussion revolvers. (This explanation is added as a special service for a few dealers who are not too quick on the trigger.)

PALM PISTOL—Something that looks more like a dispenser for roach poison than it does like a firearm. Some people collect such things.

PARADOX GUN—Something intended to be used either as a scattergun or as a slug gun. The bore is smooth except near the muzzle where it has rifling. This weapon antedates the rifled slug. It worked surprisingly well; it threw a devastating projectile and could be brought into action far more quickly than horse-drawn artillery.

PATCH—Paper or cloth covering for bullet.

PATCH BOX—Storage compartment for bullet patches found on many early rifles. There is a legend about somebody's finding a rare gold coin in a patch box. (I have, myself, found remains of a few dead spiders, but usually there is nothing there but a musty odor.) Instructions for opening these cavities do not always come with the rifle, but a novice can usually accomplish the feat by prying with a screwdriver. In case of extreme emergency, dynamite is recommended.

PATERSON—Town in New Jersey; home of Patent Arms Mfg. Co. (none other than Colt). Also a revolver or rifle made there. Also an expert on gun collecting on the staff of the National Rifle Association, C(harles) Meade Patterson.

PENNSYLVANIA—A term which a few enthusiasts of this state would like to substitute for KENTUCKY as a designation for a fullstock, flintlock rifle. See LANCASTER and you will begin to understand how the business fits together. They are confused.

PEPPERBOX—An early type of revolver in which the cylinder and barrels are integral. A contemporary

testimonial on the efficiency of these weapons is
given by Mark Twain in *Roughing It*. He apparently does not understand the advantage of having
the front sights in motion during the process of pulling the trigger—if, indeed, the thing has any front
sights. (See Plate I.)

PINFIRE—A type of cartridge ignition used on guns
of European origin. See CARTRIDGES.

PINWHEEL—A shot centered in the 10-ring of a
target.

PLAIN—A plainly finished rifle which usually sold
for less than an ornate one. Usually a halfstock
rifle.

PLAINS—A term arising from the erroneous supposition that "plain" means "plains," and therefore a
rifle used on the plains. Here again there is no
evidence as to who the joker was who first added the
"s." He was probably attempting to make a cheap
rifle sound high powered in his description.

PLINKER—A casual shooter of the at-tomato-cans
variety. There is an expression to describe the at-
highway-markers shooter, but it cannot be included
here.

POINT—Something idiots do with firearms toward
friends—a practice which should be left exclusively
to bird dogs.

POLYGROOVE—Type of rifling with many grooves, serving the dubious purpose of letting gas escape around the bullet.

PROOF MARKS—Small, more-or-less discernible marks placed on European guns by certain authorized "houses." Similar types of marks, of more recent origin, are placed on some American arms by their manufacturers. Early American military arms show proof marks, and some early manufacturers—particularly Deringer—used proof marks of their own. See *Proof Tests and Proof Marks* by Goddard.

PYRITE—An iron sulfide mineral used for making sparks, as in a wheel-lock gun.

RECONVERSION—A legal operation only when done in order to obtain a "shooter." One of the principal vocations of the unscrupulous basement mechanic. Also a rifle so altered from percussion back to flintlock.

REMINGTON—Famous firearms maker. Also a pistol, revolver, rifle, or shotgun made by same. See *Remington Handguns* by Karr and Karr. Also famous painter of Westerns.

REVOLVER—A pistol that discharges hot gases, and occasionally a little lead, from the junction between the cylinder and the barrel. However, it has sights that remain stationary, which is more than can be said for most semiautomatic pistols. Erroneously, it is popularly believed to have been invented by Colt —presumably while under the influence of his own nitrous oxide. (See Plates III and IV.)

RIFLE—A long gun with a barrel which has lands and grooves, or which had lands and grooves, or which should have lands and grooves. Some Kentucky "rifles" do not have rifled barrels and there is reason to believe that grooves were not cut in their bores.

ROMAN NOSE—Type of stock occasionally seen on flintlock rifles that has a downward curvature from the comb to the heel.

ROOT—A percussion Colt with an outside or side hammer. This is one of the few Colt models that is identified with the name of anybody other than Colt. Were it not publicly attributed to Root, one might be inclined to credit this model to Rube Goldberg.

RUSSIAN—A native of the U.S.S.R. More likely in gun circles a Smith & Wesson model manufactured for the Russian Government before Russia became a democracy. A relatively few Russians were stamped with the manufacturer's name in English. Those actually exported were all supposedly stamped with the Russian transliteration of the maker's name, address, etc. (If you ever stumble onto one of these, you will probably recognize it. I did, even more years ago than I care to admit.)

SCATTERGUN—Usually applies to a shotgun, but some rifles and pistols could certainly claim this distinction.

SERIAL NUMBER—Something that had better be intact on a modern gun. One of the things often "doctored" on certain types of antiques. See also: MIXED NUMBERS and ASSEMBLY NUMBERS.

SET TRIGGER—A trigger to trigger another trigger to trigger the sear.

SHARPS—Another fellow who spent some time in the City of Brotherly Love. Many small four-barrel pistols bear his name, as well as some fine sporting rifles and military rifles and carbines.

SHARPSHOOTER—Somebody wandering through a junk shop trying to discover a dragoon priced at ten dollars.

SHOOTER—A rifle or pistol that might otherwise be a collector's piece, but is used or presumably could be used for shooting. Note particularly that the word "shooter" in an ad does not imply any liability on the part of the dealer if you blow your head off, and many dealers explicitly say so. Others appear to have no imagination whatever.

Signal Pistol—A gigantic, awkward-looking piece of junk occasionally seen in the "collection" of somebody who knows nothing about gun collecting. One would not suppose so many of these things existed until he has advertised to buy antique guns, and driven a few miles to see them on a cold winter's night.

Sitting Bull—The chap who gave Custer such a hard time at the Little Big Horn.

Sitting Duck—Anything that is about to be clobbered, but not necessarily something with webbed feet.

Slag—A hard inclusion sometimes found in the metal of rifle barrels.

Smith & Wesson—They are still operating under the same name, and started some time ago. See book by McHenry and Roper, *Smith & Wesson Handguns*.

Sporter—Frequently means a military rifle with new or altered stock. Anything or everything else may be different too, including the barrel. Can also mean a manufacturer's product with certain features similar to a model commonly supplied as a target rifle, as for example, a Winchester Model 52 Sporter.

Springfield—A government armory in Massachusetts. Also a military rifle made there—or anywhere else, including the Rock Island Arsenal, for that matter. "Springfields" include various types of ignition as well as calibers from .22 to .69. The term is used in the same vague sense as GUN, which see.

SQUIRREL RIFLE—A muzzle-loading rifle that somebody thinks might have been used for shooting squirrels because of its small caliber. The designation has dubious merit; I suggest as a substitute: racoon-hunting rifle for obtaining 'coon tails for decorating caps of 'coon hunters.

STARTER—A device for introducing a bullet into the muzzle without causing deformation of the bullet. A starter pistol is a blank-cartridge pistol used for adding to the excitement of track meets and other sports events.

SUICIDE SPECIAL—Any of various revolvers of uncertain quality, whose manufacturers did not normally mark their products with their names, but used instead some trade name like: Bulls-Eye, Napoleon, Tramp's Terror, Blue Whistler, Smoker, and at least a hundred similar aliases. Some people collect these things. I collect information about them, which may be more valuable than the revolvers themselves. (See Plate VII.)

TAPE PRIMER—Type of ignition invented by MAYNARD, which see.

TEAT PRIMER—Type of primer used on a metallic cartridge which was loaded into the revolving cylinder from the front.

TEXAS—A portion of Mexico that became a republic in spite of some misunderstandings on the matter. Also a model of Colt revolver that was used in arriving at an understanding.

TIGER STRIPE—A striped texture or grain of wood, frequently maple, used for stocks of flint and percussion rifles.

TIT FIRE—Cartridge identical with that described under TEAT PRIMER, or a pistol using such a cartridge.

T-MAN—Representative of the U.S. Treasury Department, the agency that licenses dealers under the Federal Firearms Act.

TUBE—Synonymous with NIPPLE, which see.

UNDER HAMMER—Nothing's under the hammer—the hammer and nipple are underneath the barrel.

UNITED STATES PROPERTY—If you are on good terms with numerous attorneys, you might collect some examples so marked. With or without this marking, don't collect anything with the serial number removed.

VENT—A hole at the breech of percussion rifles allegedly to let air into the barrel and prevent the bullet from creating a vacuum as it progresses down the bore. This theory seems to be of English or Continental origin because very few American rifles are equipped with vents, among the few exceptions being a rifle manufactured by J. Abendshen, Pittsburgh, about 1860, and it may have been on special order. Supposedly the Americans didn't understand this "vacuum" theory. The vent seems to be a hangover from the touch hole of the flintlock.

VOLCANIC—Any of several models of lever-action repeating pistols manufactured by the Volcanic Repeating Arms Co. or New Haven Arms Co. under Smith & Wesson patents. These arms are the forerunners of the Henry and Winchester lever-action rifles.

WACKY—My son's bird dog.

WALKER—A colonel in U.S. Army for whom an early Colt model is affectionately named by collectors.

WAR BETWEEN THE STATES—A struggle that is likely to continue for some time, although the fighting will probably continue with words rather than gunfire. Persons who have never crossed the Mason-Dixon Line believe this is synonymous with the Civil War.

The ABC of It

WATERS, ASA—Contractor who manufactured flint-lock pistols for U.S. Government.

WELLS FARGO—An express company that operated overland stagecoaches. The arms issued to their employees were usually marked, thus any arms so marked. A term sometimes applied to a particular model of percussion Colt—by the Colt collectors, but not by the Express Company which also issued Remingtons, *et al.*

WHEEL-LOCK—Type of ignition system involving a windup wheel that made sparks by rubbing against pyrite. This ingenious mechanism replaced the matchlock system, in general, and preceded the flintlock.

WHITNEY—Fellow with first name of Eli, inventor of gin, manufacturer of firearms.

WHITNEYVILLE—*Chez* Whitney. Also a Colt manu-factured by Eli during Colt's momentary embar-rassment of having a government contract but no capital equipment and nobody but Salesman Sam working for him.

WILD BILL—Name of a frontiersman, James Butler Hickok, 1837–76.

WINDY CITY — Robbers'-Town-on-Lake-Michigan, birthplace of the author. The Indian name, Chicago, is supposed to mean big swamp or place where the

117

skunk cabbage grows. Original location of Fort Dearborn.

WORKING ORDER—Term used by dealers to describe arms on which most of the parts are free to move after having been saturated with penetrating oil or kerosene.

WORM—Something that turns. If on the end of a ramrod, it supposedly will engage itself in a musket ball and permit extraction thereof—at least that's the theory.

ZEBRA—A sport model jackass. Sometimes applied to two-legged animals that fit this description.

ZULU—A piece of junk in the form of a shotgun usually assembled in Europe from miscellaneous parts, including musket locks. These choice items are occasionally seen on the American market at offering prices around a hundred times what they are worth. Some dealers claim these are excellent pieces for starting a collection, but I think they are better for ending it.

CHAPTER 7

He ground and filed, and sweat a lot,
And bent the metal while it was hot.
He quenched it then in melted lard,
But, even so, it wasn't hard;
Bye and bye, he began to feel
Perhaps the metal wasn't steel.

—WAS EISEN

How Not to Repair Guns— An Added Attraction

ALTHOUGH the price of the book is undoubtedly justifiable on the basis of this chapter alone, this chapter requires some justification, at least in quantitative terms. In the first place, it is my opinion that there are some individuals who shouldn't attempt to repair guns. To put it in polite terms: their talents are more highly developed along other lines, such as reading books—particularly this one—or watching TV. Nevertheless, anybody who can drive a nail and hang a picture without demolishing a noticeable segment of the wall has *some* talent as a gunsmith. It is my concern here to give artisans of this group some advice on what not to do. Others should continue to read books and watch TV. Having mentioned only one tool, the hammer, I must hasten to explain that driving of nails is not a recommended procedure for the repair of firearms in general. So if you had already taken out your hammer and some nails, put them away. You can search for them again later—after Junior comes home and recalls where he has left them.

Expensive power tools for working with wood and metal make an excellent display for impressing one's friends but are not necessary for most amateur gunsmithing jobs. In fact, if it is assumed that most percussion rifles can be repaired with equipment no more complicated than the machinery used in their original manufacture, something far less than a complete, modern machine shop will suffice. Personally I have been able to handle the average job with a few hand tools and a motor-driven mandrel which will take a chuck and a small grinding wheel, wire brush, buffers, etc. This is not a particularly good substitute for a drill press or a lathe, but it is adequate for working on small parts.

One of the most frequent ailments of handguns is

a broken spring. Percussion firearms frequently have badly corroded nipples. Revolvers may have a damaged pawl or pawl spring, but the trigger or bolt spring is frequently nonfunctional. What to do?

Let's start at the beginning. First of all, find out whether the arm is loaded. For percussion arms this cannot always be ascertained from casual inspection, except for the usual type of revolver. The bore of any other firearm should be completely opened so that air can be blown in from the muzzle and come out through the nipple. This means that the nipple must be opened —for which purpose I use an "Allways" saw blade. This is a cylindrical steel wire with cutting ridges on it. There is virtually no possibility of breaking this off inside of the nipple.

An old load can be shot out of a pistol, rifle or shotgun provided the gun appears to be in good condition and provided it is safe to assume that the gun was properly loaded with a *safe charge of black powder.* If there is any possibility that it could be loaded with smokeless powder, don't shoot it. Under any circumstances do not hold a rifle or shotgun while an old load is being discharged. Prop it up with the butt against a large tree and fire it with a string while standing behind the tree. Needless to say, this operation is not ideally suited to the back yard of an urban residence, unless you wish to replace your neighbor's automobile. You are strictly on your own, of course. I know of no insurance company that will assume the risk of what an individual is likely to do with a firearm under such circumstances.

Pistols and revolvers can be discharged indoors. The principal hazard here may be a woman's wrath or it may be the firearm. Protection against the latter can be had by standing behind a wooden door and extending the arm around it in such a manner that only the hand and forearm are exposed. The bullet should be discharged into scrap wood or other suitable stopping material. Care must be taken that a ricochet is not possible, either in your direction or through a window. I have no suggestions regarding the wife's wrath, but have discovered that the repercussions are less severe if she is warned in advance or if she is out of the house at the time.

These statements apply, naturally, to percussion arms rather than cartridge arms. If you run onto a cartridge arm and can't determine whether it is loaded, don't handle any part of it—particularly the trigger. And above all don't cock the hammer. These may seem like unnecessarily naïve comments, but I can assure you that these comments are not as naïve as some persons that handle guns. None less than a Deputy

Police Chief shot himself through the hand with a Sharps 4-barrel pistol, which is now in my possession. I wasn't there at the time but I can visualize the probable sequence of events. The barrels on this particular model slide forward while pressure is applied to a button, but only when the hammer is at half cock. Our friend probably tried it with the hammer forward and then with the hammer all the way back. Whoops, one bullet through the left hand. Some people find learning more difficult than others.

Semiautomatic pistols are the worst of the lot, but I shall not waste any of my pearls of wisdom on these swine. They are not ordinarily considered collectors' items. A few hardy souls collect such things and they probably have their own trade secrets for not putting bullets through their heads—although, on at least one occasion, I heard of a case in which one of these renegades almost put a bullet through the head of somebody else.

After the barrel is found to be unloaded, a good cleaning is almost always in order. One of the best solvents for anything likely to be present is hot water and a little diluted household ammonia. For rifles and shotguns it is frequently desirable to remove the nipple and sometimes the breech plug. If a good penetrating oil will not free the nipple, and it is in poor condition, it can be removed by heating. This will ruin the hardness of the nipple, but it wasn't any good anyway. Frequently the breech plug as well as the nipple can be removed after heating to a dull red over the gas burner of a domestic furnace. Sometimes enough heat can be obtained from the burner of a gas cooking range, but usually not.

Shotgun double barrels should not be heated to free the breech plugs. The barrels are usually welded together with a solder that has a comparatively low melting temperature. The barrels look much nicer fastened together than they do separated, so I do not supply any instructions for putting them back together, but merely the precaution not to separate them in the first place.

Percussion rifles frequently have thimbles missing. Iron thimbles can be turned from quarter-inch gas pipe if one has a lathe or a friend who has a lathe. Brass thimbles can be duplicated or sometimes purchased. They are soldered to the rib with a tin-lead solder. This involves heating the barrel in this region and keeping other portions cool so as not to unsolder anything else. These operations can usually be accomplished on the gas range in the kitchen, if your license to operate includes access to this portion of your castle.

The fore-end tip of a halfstock rifle is usually a

cast tin-lead mixture—at least fifty per cent tin. If missing, it is fairly easily replaced if the wood is still in good condition. Wrap a piece of aluminum foil about the fore-end so that it extends beyond where the metal should come. Place a piece of dowel, slightly larger than the ramrod, in position against the rib. Heat the solder in a lead pot on the gas range and when somewhat above the melting temperature, pour it in with the dipper that you use for casting bullets. Pour as rapidly as possible to avoid layering or seams. After the metal is flush with the rib or extends slightly beyond, you can shape the fore-end tip to suit your own fancy. Remove the barrel with care because the new tip may grasp the rib. Now shape with a bastard or coarse rasp, followed by the use of successively finer files. Finally polish with steel wool. If anybody can tell that it is not original, better luck next time. This is one of the most easily accomplished of the repair jobs that are likely to be required by a halfstock rifle.

Broken stocks are all individual problems, depending on what is missing and where the break occurs. Usually it is through the portion that includes the barrel tang. If it is almost entirely in portions that are checkered, you are lucky. This can be repaired, assuming considerable skill, in such a manner that close examination may not reveal the repair work, and the strength may be greater than it was before the break. In general, the wood is reassembled by gluing together with a urea resin glue, after all fractured surfaces have been thoroughly cleaned.

Old glue can be removed by soaking in water containing an alkaline detergent, such as "Calgonite," for ten hours or longer. When quite soft, the old glue is removed by warm water and a small brush having fairly stiff bristles. After drying for a day or two, the pieces are assembled with glue between them and are held together by tightly wound rubber tape so that the glue dries under pressure. On removal of the tape the joints should be solid, but the whole thing is a discouraging-looking mess at this stage.

Now the wood should be drilled with a long bit, starting at a concealed portion behind the breech and extending well down into the body of the stock—at least four inches beyond the break. This drilling operation should be done on a lathe or a drill press with adequate clearances, and the butt should be supported by a centered point so that nothing can slip. (The butt plate should be removed in order to accomplish this.) Thus a half-inch hole can be drilled through all of the broken wood and into undamaged wood for several inches on both sides of the fractures.

Into this is glued a half-inch birch or hickory dowel that has been slotted to permit the escape of air and excess glue. The dowel should be cut to proper dimensions before gluing, because it requires careful work to shape the end of the dowel after it is in place.

The trigger guard screws, if any, and the tang screw should penetrate into this dowel and should be lengthened, if necessary, to do so. The detergent, besides removing the old glue, will have taken off the finish on this part of the stock, so you now have a refinishing job on your hands. First, however, fill any small places where the wood is missing with stick shellac or plastic wood. Then go over the checkering with a bent three-square file. If the original checkering doesn't line up, you are in for a bad time. You shouldn't have glued it in this way. Get the checkering cleaned out so that it crosses all patches in the checkered area, and darken the checkered cuts with burnt umber or raw umber in oil. Finally, refinish the stock, using any of the approved methods, or any better method about which you may have special knowledge.

My only universal ingredient for stock refinishing is plenty of patience—something that can't be bought at any store. Water-soluble dyes, varnish, boiled linseed oil, several oil pigments, shellac and various other

materials are used. Bad breaks that involve additions
of plastic wood cannot be finished light without giving an unsightly appearance. Under these circumstances the repair work, usually adjacent to the lock,
must be darkened in such a way that it can grade into
light-colored areas of the fore-end and comb. On occasions I have used a dark-brown paint for this purpose, and the painted portion has been made to blend
with the rest of the finish. This sounds like the wildest
kind of fabrication, and persons have examined such
examples without believing what they saw. I have
only one secret: a small amount of time every few
days, spread out over weeks or even months.

Some persons are quite surprised to discover that
some of the fancy-burl walnut stocks of fine English
shotguns contain patches, plugs or inserts. This sort
of assembly is not too difficult in dark wood like walnut, but it is really tricky for a light-colored wood,
such as ash or maple. In general, I finish rifle and
shotgun stocks with one or two coats of spar varnish,
rubbing each coat smooth with fine steel wool. After-
wards several coats of boiled oil are applied, allowing
a week or more for each coat to harden. If a glossy
surface is desired a French polish is applied. Before
starting on such a project, a person should be certain
of three to five hours without interruption. If done

properly, this is real work, so I therefore recommend it as an excellent way not to refinish stocks.

Only one additional remark will be made about woodworking. Although chisels are traditional for inletting, a high-speed hand grinder can be used for this purpose in some instances. If patches are necessarily added to a stock and they extend into the recess for the lock, this situation can frequently be remedied in a few seconds with a cylindrical cutting burr. Due respect should be maintained for these burrs when revolving at about 20,000 r.p.m. What they will do to wood, they will do more readily to human flesh. Nevertheless, such a tool is highly effective for sculpturing pistol grips of wood or ivory, and will work satisfactorily for shaping a tin-lead fore-end tip.

Metal work on guns is fully as fascinating as woodwork. Locks frequently need repairs. The secret, if any secret there is, consists of being able to find a piece of metal from which the desired part can be cut with the least amount of effort. Most of the cutting is done either by grinding or filing, but drilling and tapping are sometimes necessary. The most difficult part of the operation frequently consists of devising a means for holding the d— thing in the vise while working on it.

Under all conditions I follow one guiding principle: never remove any metal without being certain what the ultimate effect is going to be. Metal is much easier to remove than to put back, so don't take off too much. You may find it quite inconvenient to start again from scratch. If you contemplate working on locks, you should have a collection of miscellaneous tumblers, sears, bridles, etc., that can be utilized with only minor alterations. You should also have a method of rehardening most of these parts after altering them, because the hardened surface layer may be removed during the process of alteration.

Small flat springs are always a source of considerable annoyance when missing or broken. They can be made from annealed spring stock by filing or grinding and then hardened and tempered. Some spring steels cannot be bent cold but must be given their curvature at a dull-red heat. This can frequently be done over the flame of a gas range, but care must be exercised not to burn the steel by heating it too hot, or too long. After one is satisfied that the proper shape has been attained, the entire spring is raised to a cherry-red color and quenched in oil—cottonseed oil or ordinary cooking oil will work. Next the temper is drawn by holding the spring just above the kindling temperature of the oil until the oil burns off. Now try it. If it breaks, it was too hard. Make another one.

How Not to Repair Guns

If that breaks also, try another piece of steel. If the third one breaks also, set the thing aside for a few weeks, and don't try another until you are in such a humor that you don't care whether it breaks or not.

Milady's toilet is not obviously related to repair of firearms, but bobby pins can be altered to make excellent flat springs of small dimensions. Also the springs in certain types of hair curlers can be fashioned into trigger springs under favorable circumstances. This is elegant—when it will work. I fear, in anticipation, receiving a letter from an irate reader informing me that he has attempted to make a main spring for a military revolver from a bobby pin, and demanding that he be refunded the price of the book. Therefore I shall say nothing further about the inimical subject of springs. Enough may already be too much on this topic.

Amateur gunsmithing can be more fun if two or three people go at it together. They can sort of work at it like a committee—pooling their ignorance, so to speak. This system worked exceedingly well in Denver.

Three of us frequently worked together in a basement on Ivy Street. What went on in this basement is difficult to recall in detail, but it included recutting rifle barrels, among other things. A fourth chap named

Burt often showed up to see what was under way at the moment. Sometimes he brought refreshments with him. One night he brought a fifth of tequila, a distilled product from the fermentation of the maguey cactus—needles and all, one would gather. I had previously struck up a mild acquaintance in Texas with this brand of fire water, which smells like a mixture of wood alcohol and kerosene, but had not been introduced to the ritual which accompanies drinking it out of the bottle. Burt demonstrated the several steps involved. A quarter of a lemon is held between the index finger and thumb of the left hand, and a salt shaker in the right hand. One moistens the fleshy part of the back of his left hand (without releasing his grasp on the lemon) with his tongue. He now sprinkles salt on it, sets down salt shaker and picks up fifth. He transfers salt from back of hand to mouth, takes swig out of bottle and squeezes lemon in mouth. Or maybe the lemon comes first, I don't seem to remember. This process can be repeated until bottle is empty or until the supply of salt and lemons dwindles. The entire treatment, on a scale comparable to Burt's little party, should be repeated at intervals of about once every thirty years.

Earlier, the gift from Mr. Thomas, the shotgun with square-back trigger guard and the cherry stock, was mentioned. What the "awful three" did to this never should be done to any shotgun. The stock was repaired by adding a large piece of matching cherry. The barrels were cut off at the breech and new plugs were made. New drums were inserted to support new nipples. The locks were rebuilt, and the barrels were refitted to the stock. It was proof fired to make certain that everything was perfect, and later sold to a friend in Pittsburgh for $7.50. Considering the number of man-hours that went into this project, I would guess that we earned between ten and fifteen cents an hour for our efforts.

One of the most unsightly features of an antique pistol may be the heads of the screws. If possible, it is best to replace Colt screws. Most varieties of such screws can be purchased from dealers who advertise in *The American Rifleman* and elsewhere. If the heads are not too badly damaged, they can be peened to straighten the slots and then cut down a few thousandths of an inch. The chuck on my mandrel serves as a lathe for this purpose. The cutting is done with a file. The screw is finally polished and blued.

Screws that are excessively tight should be loosened by application of penetrating oil and by tapping with a brass hammer or brass rod. If the screw goes through the frame, this treatment should be applied at both ends. Because heat should not be applied to hardened parts or springs, it is usually not practicable to heat the entire mechanism prior to disassembly.

In general, major alterations to firearms are regarded with suspicion by collectors, and may destroy much of the article's original value. Refinishing of metal parts falls within the category of what ordinarily should not be done. Replacement of a percussion lock with a flint lock—that is, reconversion—definitely falls in the classification of faking. Words can hardly describe what is thought of some of the birds that manufacture Walker model Colts from dragoon parts. I have heard it suggested that their fathers were probably horse thieves, and some uncomplimentary things may even have been implied about their mothers.

Lock, Stock and Barrel

CHAPTER 8

I shoot a shot,
And brag a lot,
But do not care
To meet a bear.
—A. PLINKER

If You Are Also a Shooter, You've Had It

ALTHOUGH I cannot verify the truth of my assumption, I have a theory that shooting may be as old as firearms. I worked this out on my own time, so to speak, so if it contains any patentable ideas I am, nevertheless, free to discuss the matter and under no obligation to make an assignment of my claims. What psychological impulse creates the fascination for shooting I cannot say, but at least two factors are of importance according to my analysis. Small boys enjoy shooting off firecrackers. Older boys enjoy the report of a pistol, rifle or shotgun.

Another facet seems to involve the instinctive urge to break something, such as a clay pigeon or a bottle. Punching holes in paper targets with bullets is a milder expression of this mania, but the same psychological release mechanisms are undoubtedly involved. Writers, if I am not presumptive in judging from my own reactions, find a certain inward satisfaction in violently crumpling a piece of paper and hurling it into the wastebasket. I have recently acquired skill in this aspect of preparing a book.

Then, again, there is sometimes a desire to do something a little bit better than the next fellow, even if it merely amounts to making holes in a piece of paper that is so far away that one can hardly see it. Having done something that seems slightly difficult, it then becomes necessary to describe it in such a manner as to preserve an element of plausibility and still make it sound almost impossible. The fisherman has his own ruses. So does the hunter. And finally, the shooter has his.

I went deer hunting in Wyoming several years ago with a muzzle-loading rifle and badly frightened a five-point buck—at least he didn't wait around for me to reload, a process that takes about two minutes. I did clobber a large snowshoe rabbit on this expedition—much to the amusement of the rest of the party.

The night before this hunt began, the guests were checking in at the ranch house and chatting briefly with the rancher. He had hunted almost everything found on the North American continent, as was obvious from the trophies on the walls and floor of his game room. Three coyote skins caught the eye of one of the dudes, a physician from Denver. In something less than his best bedside manner he observed that the coyote skins appeared somewhat incongruous as a part of the exhibits. True to Western tradition, nobody informed the medical man that these were albino coyotes, or what might be the probability of his ever seeing one—much less shooting it. I had never seen one before and had inquired why the skins were unusually light colored.

One of the principals of this junket was Ed Hunter, who wrote the hunting and fishing column of the *Denver Post* (elsewhere deliberately referred to as *Pest*). He was known as "One-shot, One-fish Hunter," partly because of his organization of the antelope hunts in which each man was allowed only one cartridge. Ed, according to reliable witnesses who always outnumbered the shooters, made a kill with a neck shot on a running antelope at two hundred and fifty yards on one such occasion. Ed certainly knew what he was doing, and I was surely in some awe-inspiring company.

Often I have wondered whether I create the impression that I know what I'm doing when out of doors or whether people enjoy pulling my leg. Bob Warren and I went on what was supposed to be his first deer hunt. He asked many questions about where to sight on the animal, how to estimate range, etc. These I cautiously answered with a few brief comments about the comparative merits of a shot in the neck *vs.* the chest, hoping that I was not in violent disagreement with some authoritative works—which I had not read. Bob said he followed my suggestions to the letter. He got a fine buck. I didn't even get a cold.

The Englewood Chapter of the Izaak Walton League had, in those days, a rifle range with target positions at fifty and a hundred yards. Much charcoal burning went on in this locality in the form of scheduled matches. At one of these affairs my friend from Wyoming (mentioned in Chapter 2) put up a purse of a hundred dollars to see if it might improve the quality of our shooting. He had another unusual habit for a shooter. This consisted of waiting until he and I had both fired two shots in a five-shot match.

On learning that I had a score of 19 or 20 to his 15 or 16, he would forthwith propose a bet that he would have a higher final score. What prompted this generosity I never learned; I didn't even consider it gambling. One day he arrived fully armed with an oriental wheel-lock gun, but that day he made no bets—not even that it would fire on the first three tries.

I have seen some of the darndest, craziest shooting. In fact, I have done some myself. At the insistence of a neighbor in Texas—an elderly lady, in fact—I once shot a cat with a pistol while the cat was moving about as fast as a cat can move. But the one that stopped me occurred on the outskirts of Denver. A neighbor and I were out plinking one afternoon, I with a single-action Army Colt and he with a Luger. Two soldiers from Lowry Field happened along and asked if we would mind if they joined us. Both were wearing **MP** armbands.

One of them was shooting hand-loaded cartridges in a .38 Special S. & W. revolver. The other had a .45 revolver. The MP with the .38 would shoot at a tomato can and get it rolling along the ground in such a way that it didn't stop while he emptied his revolver at it. My neighbor was mildly impressed. He asked the MP whether he thought he could hit a whiskey bottle that somebody had left standing erect on top of a five-gallon oil can. It was fully a hundred and seventy-five yards away and had obviously remained intact after being used as a rifle target by somebody. The MP said he might be able to hit it if given four or five shots. My neighbor looked at me and winked. The MP extended his revolver and drew a bead on something in the general vicinity of the oil can. The first shot raised dust about two inches to the left of the can at its base. The second went over the can. The third hit the whiskey bottle. All I know is, I wouldn't want him shooting at me if I were within a quarter of a mile. If he didn't hit me, he would scare me to death.

The "awful three" gunsmiths did a bit of trap-shooting with muzzle-loading shotguns. This is superior entertainment and quite inexpensive when compared with cartridge shooting. Three men make a good team. One loads while the second shoots and the third throws the targets. This sort of thing can continue all afternoon without using a pound of black powder or more than a few pounds of shot.

During the war it was difficult to obtain black powder. Once I ordered a shipment—half a keg, as I recall. The railroad agent sent me a notice that a piece of freight had arrived. I phoned to find out whether a warehouseman could arrange to remain until 5:05 P.M. in order for me to pick it up. He couldn't. The shipment couldn't be delivered a quarter of a mile beyond the delivery zone, even if it were well inside the city limits. An express company couldn't pick it up because it had been sent C.O.D. After learning all of the negative possibilities over the phone, I asked the agent if he knew what the shipment consisted of. On learning that it was black powder, he arranged for its removal from his warehouse any time before six o'clock that very evening. Mere mention of the stuff was enough to demand courteous treatment—not of me, but of the powder—from a freight agent.

Smokeless powder, on the other hand, is not particularly dangerous—until one puts it in a muzzle-loading firearm. There are a few brave souls, including me, who shoot percussion rifles with light charges of bulk smokeless powder. Why I do anything of this sort is a fair question. It's a little like opening up a modern automobile. You may find out what the safety factor is after the information is no longer of any value to you on this earth. There is certainly a risk involved, whether it is calculated or not.

Shooting of percussion revolvers is good sport. Balls or conical bullets for Colt revolvers can be cast from pure (soft) lead with Colt molds. What one uses for casting bullets for a Remington depends on the Remington. Remington handguns do not appear to have been held to close tolerances. Undersized balls can be used but, if they are, a layer of grease should be used to prevent firing the adjacent chambers from the cylinder flash. It is most disconcerting to have three chambers fire simultaneously. To this I can certify. In fact, it can be dangerous.

I have fired many types of handguns, but my strangest experience was with a derringer. This little pistol, which is almost a prototype of the pistol used by Booth to assassinate Lincoln, aroused my curiosity with respect to its shooting qualities. So I loaded it one evening and discharged it at a very green board in the basement. The ball put a respectable dent in the board, but then it bounced back and hit me in the chest. Although I sustained no wound as a consequence, after due consideration I decided not to repeat this experiment. Actually, I am not quite certain what I was trying to prove in the first place.

If, after reading this chapter, a person is still firmly resolved that he is going to become a shooter, I have a definite suggestion. He should locate in the neighborhood a shooting club that has an indoor range. (If he lives in a rural community, he may have been shooting longer than I have.) He should start with a .22 rifle, in my opinion. My sixteen-year-old son, Thomas Duncan (there's that name again), has recently made the highest qualification of the Junior Division of the National Rifle Association with a little single-shot, bolt-action Mauser rifle. Tom is now a good shot, but he has been at it for several years. To be sure, I have been coaching him with the expert advice, "Shoot as I say and not as I shoot." This is an ideal method because it permits me to retain the gratifying pride of supposing that I once knew something about shooting, a premise which in turn is predicated on a large number of correlated assumptions, many of which may never have been true.

If you are a collector of firearms, you have my sympathies. If you are also a shooter of various things —including gas pipes—you get no sympathy from me. Brother, you've had it! And you can take it with you, wherever you go!

Clay Pigeon

ANNOTATED BIBLIOGRAPHY

EXPLANATORY NOTE: By popular demand—of one person, at least—I am including a list of books that may entice my readers to delve into this business further. That is, permit them to do so on paper, without leaving the comfort of their firesides on a cold winter's night. There is no dearth of books on firearms. In fact one would have difficulty in finding a topic so specialized that an entire book has not been devoted to it. Some of these books are for experts, others are for novices, and a goodly number are for the birds.

ON HANDGUNS—ANTIQUE, MOSTLY

James E. Serven: *Colt Firearms, 1836-1954.* 385 pages. Published by the author, Santa Ana, California, 1954. A splendid book if you are ready for this many Colts to the exclusion of everything else.

John E. Parsons: *Henry Deringer's Pocket Pistol.* 255 pages. Wm. Morrow & Co., New York, 1952. A scholarly treatment of mostly percussion pistols that were manufactured mostly by one man. Well illustrated.

Charles L. Karr, Jr. and Caroll R. Karr: *Remington Handguns.* 153 pages. The Stackpole Co., Harrisburg, Pa.,

1951. Illustrated catalogue of most of the pistols and revolvers made by Remington. Besides revolvers and a semi-automatic pistol, Remington made a magazine pistol and single-shot, two-shot, four-shot, and five-shot pistols having as many barrels.

Claud E. Fuller: *The Whitney Firearms.* 335 pages. Standard Publications, Huntington, W. Va., 1946. Not too bad for so much about so little.

Arcadi Gluckman: *United States Martial Pistols and Revolvers.* 249 pages. Otto Ulbrich Co., Buffalo, N. Y., 1939. This is highly recommended for the advanced collector in this field.

Roy C. McHenry and Walter F. Roper: *Smith & Wesson Hand Guns.* 233 pages. Standard Publications, Huntington, W. Va., 1945. A fairly complete account of the affairs of this famous company.

Lewis Winant: *Pepperbox Firearms.* 188 pages. Greenberg, New York, 1952. Next probably will come separate books on three-, four-, five-, six-, and half-shot pepperboxes.

Charles E. Chapel: *Gun Collectors' Handbook of Values.* 398 pages. Coward-McCann, New York, 1955 (3rd Revised Edition). An illustrated catalogue that is useful for identification purposes. Insofar as the "values" are concerned, this book represents an attempt to accomplish the impossible. Dealers' catalogues are more realistic since the dealers hope to sell at the prices shown.

James A. Smith and Elmer Swanson: *The Antique Pistol Book.* 336 pages. Speedwell Publishing Co., Hoboken, N. J., 1948. An excellent example of what can be accomplished solely through artistic ability. Our feathered friends can have this one.

On Handguns—not so antique

Julian S. Hatcher: *Textbook of Pistols and Revolvers.* 342 pages. Thomas G. Samworth, Georgetown, S. C., 1935. This volume covers the subject admirably up to approximately the beginning of World War II.

Walter H. B. Smith: *NRA Book of Small Arms, Vol. 1—Pistols and Revolvers.* 638 pages. Military Service Publishing Co., Harrisburg, Pa., 1946. Covers arms of all countries. Well illustrated.

On Long Guns—rifles and muskets

Arcadi Gluckman: *United States Muskets, Rifles and Carbines.* 503 pages. Otto Ulbrich Co., Buffalo, N. Y., 1948. A standard reference book, based on knowledge and experience.

Ned H. Roberts: *The Muzzle-Loading Cap Lock Rifle.* 530 pages. Clark Press, Manchester, N. H., 1944 (Revised Edition, including supplement). This book covers shooting, manufacture, etc., of American non-military rifles that use percussion caps.

Walter H. B. Smith: *NRA Book of Small Arms, Vol. 2—Rifles.* 546 pages. Military Service Publishing Co., Harrisburg, Pa., 1948. An elementary treatment that is well illustrated.

James J. Grant: *Single-Shot Rifles.* 385 pages. Wm. Morrow & Co., New York, 1947. Single-shot rifles belong to an individualistic era of Americana. Data are supplied also on the diverse cartridges used in these rifles.

John G. W. Dillin: *The Kentucky Rifle.* 136 pages. Ludlum and Beebe, New York, 1946 (Third Edition). All about flintlock, fullstock rifles and their makers. The illustrations leave much to be desired.

Harold F. Williamson: *Winchester, The Gun that Won the West.* 494 pages. Combat Forces Press, Washington, D. C., 1952. Possibly the author will produce, in time, a separate volume on each individual model.

Winston O. Smith: *The Sharps Rifle.* 138 pages. Wm. Morrow & Co., New York, 1943. This title is included merely to imply that there are rifles other than Winchesters.

Joseph W. Shields, Jr.: *From Flintlock to M-1.* 220 pages. Coward-McCann, New York, 1954. Readable, historical account of the development of military muskets and rifles. Illustrated.

ON CARTRIDGES

Herschel C. Logan: *Cartridges.* 199 pages. Standard Publications, Huntington, W. Va., 1948. Excellent drawings of typical cartridges of diverse sorts, tabular information also.

Julian S. Hatcher: *Textbook of Firearms Investigation, Identification and Evidence.* (Includes also *Textbook of Pistols and Revolvers.*) 342 + 533 pages. Small-Arms Technical Publishing Co., Plantersville, N. C., 1935. Extensive data on cartridges for most modern pistols made prior to World War II, but only those commonly found in America.

H. P. White and B. D. Munhall: *Centerfire American and British Pistol and Revolver Cartridges.* 143 pages. Infantry Journal Press, Washington, D. C., 1950. Just what the title says.

See also *Single-Shot Rifles* by Grant.

On Gunsmithing

James V. Howe: *The Amateur Guncraftsman.* 313 pages. Funk & Wagnalls, New York, 1943. A good place to start to learn to tinker.

J. P. Stelle and William B. Harrison: *The Gunsmith's Manual.* 376 pages. Excelsior Publishing House, New York, 1883. (Reprinted by Thomas G. Samworth, Georgetown, N. C., 1945.) Hand workmanship hasn't changed much in the past seventy years.

James V. Howe: *The Modern Gunsmith.* Two vols., 941 pages. Funk & Wagnalls, New York, 1945 (Revised Edition). "The most authoritative work ever written. . . ." See next title.

Roy F. Dunlap: *Gunsmithing.* 800 pages. Thomas G. Samworth, Georgetown, S. C., 1950. ". . . the most complete ever written. . . ." Pay your money and take your choice of either of these or of many others, the titles of which include such words as simplified, professional, elementary, advanced, etc.

Annotated Bibliography

ON SHOOTING—LEARNING TO SHOOT, THAT IS

Note: You might just as well read a book on how to skip rope or how not to boil a teakettle dry as to read a book and expect to learn how to shoot. Books on shooting are so numerous that it has become almost necessary to specify the caliber and the barrel length in order to come up with a new title.

The National Rifle Association publishes some inexpensive handbooks with the following titles:

> *Shooting the .22 Rifle*
> *Pistol Marksmanship*
> *Hunter's Manual*
> *Small Arms Ballistics*

These are highly recommended. For hundreds of other books on shooting see *Guns and Shooting* by Riling.

Ed McGivern: *Ed McGivern's Book on Fast and Fancy Revolver Shooting and Police Training.* 484 pages. King Richardson Co., Springfield, Mass., 1938. An amazing account of what can be done with a modern, double-action revolver as contrasted with what allegedly was done by fanning the single-action revolver long years ago.

K. Zimmermann: *Die Schiesskunst; ein Lehrbuch zum Selbsunterricht für Standschutzen, Soldaten und Jäger.* 416 pages. Luzern, 1942. Dose 'oo t'shut learnen vollen, heer finden ein goot Buck auf Deutsch geprintet. Ain't? (Recommended for Pennsylvanians.)

Annotated Bibliography

ET CETERA

Ray Riling: *The Powder Flask Book.* 514 pages. Robert Halter, New Hope, Pa., 1953. A powder flask is a powder flask is a powder flask. Beautiful illustrations of more than 1,500 varieties.

Herschel C. Logan: *Hand Cannon to Automatic.* 172 pages. Standard Publications, Huntington, W. Va., 1944. A primer on the history of firearms, contains 172 illustrative plates.

Arcadi Gluckman and L. D. Satterlee: *American Gun Makers.* 243 pages. The Stackpole Co., Harrisburg, Pa., 1953 (Revised Edition). A directory of gun makers, including some on whom very little information is available.

A. Merwyn Carey: *American Firearms Makers.* 146 pages. Thomas Y. Crowell Co., New York, 1953. Another attempt, among several, to give us the latest word on the earliest gunsmiths.

Claud E. Fuller and Richard D. Steuart: *Firearms of the Confederacy.* 333 pages. Standard Publications, Huntington, W. Va., 1944. Highly specialized, but interesting.

Paul Wahl: *The Gun Trader's Guide.* 225 pages. Greenberg, New York, 1953. With this book the neophyte becomes an expert overnight. If you believe this, send me a postal card with your name and address on it—I may want to dispose of some gold bricks someday.

John E. Parsons and John S. du Mont: *Firearms in the Custer Battle.* 59 pages. The Stackpole Co., Harrisburg, Pa., 1953. No library on firearms would be complete without

Annotated Bibliography

this volume, but I have never seen a complete library on firearms and never hope to see one.

Calvin H. Goddard: *Proof Tests and Proof Marks.* 26 pages. Reprinted articles from *Army Ordnance,* Army Ordnance Association, Washington 6, D. C., 1933–1934. Proof marks used prior to World War II, including those of U. S. government armories.

The American Rifleman. Published monthly by the National Rifle Association, Washington 6, D. C. This magazine frequently contains articles on some subject other than hand loading of wildcat cartridges.

Muzzle Blasts. Published monthly by the National Muzzle Loading Rifle Association, P. O. Box 1150, Portsmouth, Ohio. A few articles and many ads.

Ray Riling: *Guns and Shooting.* 434 pages. Greenberg, New York, 1951. Here is a bibliography to end all bibliographies—including this one.

Postlude

I shall be terse
In one more verse;
No more offend—
This is *the end.*

    –YOURS TRULY